MW01106636

The Best of
retirehappyblog

#1 Voted BEST Personal Finance Blog
in Canada by the Globe and Mail

Take Control
of Your Money

Authors:
Jim Yih
Sarah Milton

Think Box Consulting

Cover Design: Jim Yih
Editor: Sarah Milton

The Best of Retire Happy Blog
Copyright © 2014 Think Box Consulting Inc. and Jim Yih

For information, address: Think Box, 7614-119 Street, Edmonton, Alberta Canada. T6G 1W3 | www.RetireHappy.ca

FIRST EDITION
Printed in Canada

100% to Charity

Special thanks go out to Clearpoint Benefit Solutions for sponsoring this book. Clearpoint is one of Western Canada's leading Group Benefit consultants. One of the core values of Clearpoint Benefit Solutions is to give back to the community through charitable endeavours. Clearpoint is proud to sponsor the Take Control of Your Money book to help employers and employees by promoting more financial awareness and wellness.

100% of the proceeds of the book will be donated to charity. We are proud to support the Edmonton Community Foundation and specifically the YIH Charitable Giving Fund.

Your support will help support charities in our community that help children, because they represent our future.

Thank you!

Jim & Sarah

About the Authors

Google **Jim Yih** and you will see that he has extensive media coverage and a significant web presence. As a professional financial speaker, best-selling author, syndicated columnist and financial expert, Jim is passionate about financial education and helping people make better decisions with money.

Jim uses his 20 years of experience in the financial industry to help people demystify investing, retirement and personal finance. His passion to educate is seen in his relentless development of financial education tools, resources and products including audio CDs and software programs. To hire Jim for your next function visit www.JimYih.com.

Sarah Milton has been in the financial industry since 2010 and has been writing a weekly post for Retire Happy since 2012.

With several years' experience in financial services and a talent for speaking, writing and teaching, Sarah is passionate about inspiring people to get excited about their money. She works alongside Jim to bring Group Retirement Programs into the workplace and support new and existing clients. Sarah is committed to building long-term client relationships and delivering quality financial education sessions that empower people to take control of their financial future and enable them to achieve their goals.

Throughout the book, you will also find articles contributed by other authors from the RetireHappy Blog. We would like to thank and acknowledge **Tricia French, Scott Wallace, Glenn Cooke, Cathy Leahy** and **Peter Merrick** for their contributions to the Take Control of Your Money book.

About Retire Happy

RetireHappy.ca is an award-winning site that publishes top quality, timeless financial planning information. RetireHappy.ca has been recognized many times by some of the top financial resources and publications like the Globe and Mail and Moneysense as one of Canada's best resources for retirement, financial planning, investing and estate planning.

There are many other financial and investing sites that focus on minute-by-minute investment ideas, changing markets and fast pace trends. As the old saying goes, *"Give a man a fish and he eats for a day. Teach a man to fish and he eats for a lifetime"*. RetireHappy.ca is a site that focuses on practical, timeless information that is intended to make a lifetime difference instead of a five minute difference.

We understand the power of the reader and we want to make sure that we deliver information that people want to know. To achieve this we have created a site that is easy to use and where the reader can easily find the information they want. We encourage interaction and comments because we believe that we can all learn from each other.

RetireHappy.ca is about bringing experts and people who want information together. We strive to be the site that everyone thinks of if they need good quality financial planning information.

Introduction

Let's be honest. Everyone wants to be financially better off than where they are today. We believe you have the ability to make that happen no matter who you are. Whether you make it happen hinges on one question, "how badly do you want it?"

The basic goal of this book is to give you some timeless insights into how to take control of your money and your financial affairs so you can become wealthier, more financially secure and achieve whatever you hope to achieve financially. Money can control your life or you can control your money. We believe that having control of your money is the better solution.

Personal finance is a big topic and there is no shortage of books and information available on it. Our professional life has been dedicated to helping others achieve more success, wealth and happiness by taking control of their financial habits.

About This Book

Take Control of Your Money is really a collection of great ideas. In fact you could call it our best ideas; ideas on how to take control of your money.

The articles are written not only by us but also a team of professionals who have written for RetireHappy.ca over the past 20 years.

The articles are in no particular order but they are grouped into some key personal finance themes or topics. The beauty of the book is, because the articles focus on key ideas to help you take control of your money you don't have to read the chapters in a specific order. Just dip in and see what resonates with you.

It's all about finding your own "Light bulb moments"

Contents

GENERAL FINANCE

"It ain't what you don't know that gets you into trouble. It's what you know for sure that just ain't so."

MARK TWAIN

Take Control of Your Money
by Jim Yih

For many, times have been tough. We've gone through many significant downturns in the stock market. As a result, many investors have become disillusioned with the stock market as a solid investment vehicle for their retirement savings. And who can blame them? Economically, we are seeing the effects of a society that continues to consume and spend money they don't have. The growing debt crisis is a real problem and it is hitting us straight in the face.

What Do We Do About Tough Times?

In tough times, we need words of encouragement but, more importantly, it's in tough times that we need to take control of our money so that we can emerge from them a winner. Tough times test our fortitude, our drive and our resilience. Those that can persevere through these times will reap the benefits as the economy and stock market turn for the better. Whether you are an individual, a business, an organization or even the government, it is the tough times that really test quality. I've always said quality is not about how you do in good times but rather, how you do in bad times.

Tough times remind us how important some of the core philosophies about wealth and money are. Navigating tough times successfully is all about taking control of your money and your life and taking the necessary actions to improvement.

1. Get Your Financial House In Order.

My wife is a dietician and she always says to me "If you want to lose weight, you need to start by looking at your life and assessing your habits and lifestyle to see where the root of the problem is."

This common sense message is just as applicable to finances as it is to weight loss. In order to take control of your money, you first need to know where you stand financially. To do so, you need to take stock of your situation by figuring out your net worth. Your net worth is like your own personal balance sheet: you list the value of what you own and what you owe and hopefully the difference between the two totals (your worth) is not negative. Whatever your number; it serves as your starting point for measuring wealth.

Knowing your net worth isn't enough on its own; you also need to know how much you spend. How will you know if you are overspending or not if you don't track your spending in some way, shape or form? Some people might assume this is where budgeting comes into play. Not me. I don't like the word 'budgeting', just like I don't like the word 'dieting', because they both imply restriction of natural behaviour. I'm not suggesting everyone needs to budget but I am suggesting that everyone needs to know how much money is spent each and every month. If tracking your spending reveals that you have a spending problem, then it makes sense to budget your money in the same way that, if you have an eating problem, then it makes sense to diet.

Successful people live within their means but how can you do that if you don't know what your means is costing you? Take the time to figure out how much money you spend and then invest time to make tracking your spending a regular habit. I promise you it will go a long way towards securing your financial future.

2. Pay Down Debts.

We live in a society that has way too much debt. Everywhere we turn it is remarkably easy to access lines of credit, credit cards and bigger mortgages as well as all kinds of "buy now, pay later" financing options.

My 82-year-old father, like many of his generation, is debt adverse. When I think back to when I was growing up I can remember so clearly him saying, "We can't buy it because we don't have the CASH." Today, we all use a different language that promotes instant gratification, "We can buy it as long as we can afford the PAYMENTS." 'Buy Now. Pay Later' might have a place in moderation but it's gone too far. It's time to start paying down our debts!

The problem many people overlook when it comes to debt is that we have to earn more than a dollar in order to pay off a dollar of interest. Think about it: we all pay tax on the money we make and so, when we make a dollar, we may only get to keep 65 to 75 cents depending on our tax rate.

If the interest on your mortgage is 7%, that's the equivalent of paying 10.8% on an after-tax basis (assuming a 35% marginal tax rate). Therefore, paying off that mortgage is the equivalent of holding a guaranteed 10.8% investment. Even paying down a 5% debt is the equivalent of investing in a 7.7% GIC. Would you be happy with a 7% to 10% return? Would you move money to a GIC if it guaranteed you returns of 7% to 10%? I know I would! This is why paying off debt can be one of the best investments you ever make.

3. Know What You Are Invested In.

Investors can get frustrated when they see losses in their portfolios. Often, I get people asking me what they should do with their investments, especially when they are losing money. My response is always the same "What are you invested in?" Most people reply with "I don't know, my advisor takes care of that."

This response concerns me because I believe that nobody cares about your money more than you care about your money. Good advisors might care but they can't care more than you. Worse yet, not all advisors even care. Taking control of your money includes knowing what you are invested in. If you buy crap and you hold crap, what will you always have? (Just in case you are not sure, crap is the correct answer). So how do you know if you own crap or not if you have no idea what you own? With all the investments out there, is it possible that some of it is crap? Too much of it! Take control by finding out what you own and why you own it!

4. Pay Yourself First.

There's an old saying "To be successful, you have to save first and spend what you have left over because, if you spend first, chances are there will be nothing left at the end to save."

I've had the honour of working with a lot of financially successful people and every time I ask about how they got there, one of their key habits to success is simply the fact that they always put away a little money. Pay yourself first is a concept most people understand but don't always practice. It is such a common sense message but unfortunately, common sense is not common enough in our world.

If you're wondering how such a simple strategy works so effectively, just think about our tax system. The government figured out a long time ago that the best way to ensure that people pay their taxes is to make sure it's the first thing taken off their paycheques. "Pay Yourself First" is one of the basic strategies of financial success and the easiest way to pay yourself first is to make it automatic. David Bach, author of "The Automatic Millionaire" says, "The secret to success is to pay yourself automatically by setting up an automatic withdrawal from your bank accounts the day after you get paid."

5. Understand Taxes.

A common perception is that the ticket to wealth is to make good investment decisions. I would agree that good investment decisions might help you make better rates of return – one, two, three, four or five per cent over time but the reality is that good tax planning is far more important in building wealth than good investment planning. Making good investment decisions will certainly contribute to wealth but good tax planning can increase your financial benefit by ten, twenty, thirty or forty percent.

Taxes are a big hurdle to accumulating wealth. It seems like every time we turn around, we face some form of tax: income tax on the money we make, property tax on our homes, or sales taxes on the things we buy. As much as tax is necessary to keep the country running, I am sure that none of us want to pay more than our fair share. Effective tax planning improves our lives by ensuring we only pay what we actually owe and allowing us to put the rest of our income to work.

6. Plan For The Future

Many people spend more time planning their annual vacation than they do their financial future. Planning is an essential

15

component of financial success. Planning allows us to look ahead to the future and to put systems and strategies in place to make it as predictable as possible. For a small percentage of people financial success happens accidentally but, for most, it comes from thought, planning, direction and action.

There's an old saying that says "Any road will get you somewhere." My question is, "Is that 'somewhere' a place you want to go?" For me, planning is simply taking the time to figure out where you want to go and then taking the right path or steps to get you there. Taking the time to create wealth through intentional planning is your best chance of achieving financial success; it's not likely to happen on its own by accident.

7. Get Help

We don't do anything in life alone. Even if we're taking action by ourselves, chances are we're using information that we gained from others. Everything we learn, we learn from the world and the people around us. It is the people in our lives who shape who we are. If we want to become better with money we need to hang around people who are good with money and learn from them. These people might include:

- A financial advisor
- A financial mentor
- Your friends and family

The law of attraction says that you attract what you expect to find. If you want to be happy, hang around with happy people. If you want to be rich, hang around with rich people. If you want to be successful, hang around with successful people. I believe you are the sum of the people you hang around with and it's important to surround yourself with people who will help you succeed.

8. Engage In Your Life.

The definition of engaging is to get involved and participate. When it comes to money, you have to become accountable for how much you earn and how you spend it. Realizing this means realizing that you need to take time to monitor your money and make important decisions about your financial future. Money doesn't grow on trees (at least not at my house). Wealth doesn't magically appear. Wealth is created through hard work and that's not a bad thing. Part of the reward of financial success is knowing that you played an instrumental role in achieving it.

There's a saying that we should all learn to "WORK SMARTER, NOT HARDER". The root of this well-known saying stems from the time management industry because we all lead busy lives and finding balance has become increasingly difficult. As much as I can appreciate the message of efficiency, effectiveness and productivity, I'm not sure the saying is appropriate in the world of personal finance. I think this saying has simply created an excuse for laziness. I believe successful people WORK SMARTER AND HARDER. I've met many successful business owners and they will all tell you that success comes from hard work that often goes unnoticed. It is very rare that wealth comes without hard work.

Hard work sets the foundation for success and it can pay huge dividends. When it comes to your money, get engaged by reading more, going to workshops and seminars, and finding the right help if necessary. If you want to get ahead financially there is no substitution for participation.

How Am I Doing Financially?
by Jim Yih

The one question that everyone seems to want to know the answer to is, "How am I doing financially?" In my workshops, everyone wants to get a sense of where they stand financially. Are they in a good position? Are they failing miserably? How can they improve? Many people also want to know the answers to other questions, including:

- Am I saving enough?
- Do I have too much debt?
- Will I be able to retire?
- Do I have enough life insurance?

Comparing Yourself to Others

One of the ways to judge how well you are doing is to look at how your situation compares to other Canadians. In statistics, we call this relative benchmarking. A recent RBC report allows you to compare your financial situation to others in Canada. You can find the full report at **http://www.rbcroyalbank.com/cgi-bin/couples-and-families/comptool/start.cgi/about_yourself** but some of the key data points are summarized here:

	Singles	Couples Starting Out	Established Couples
Net Worth	$165,535	$87,841	$382,759
Income	$39,136	$76,531	$72,857
Real Estate	$240,370	$261,717	$328,409
Mortgage	$97,314	$163,357	$105,179
Credit Card	$5,342	$4,716	$6,401
Loan	$14,465	$18,948	$19,877
Line Of Credit	$26,339	$22,035	$30,741

	Families with kids under 12	Families with kids 12-18	Families with kids over 18
Net Worth	$159,973	$201,214	$279,551
Income	$77,315	$75,069	$81,371
Real Estate	$317,276	$310,987	$326,754
Mortgage	$162,283	$124,448	$118,185
Credit Card	$6,355	$6,417	$7,467
Loan	$18,398	$20,609	$19,612
Line Of Credit	$29,639	$33,084	$37,811

The data is broken down into six categories. Three of the categories benchmark against Canadians with no kids. The other three categories benchmark against those who have kids.

The Flaw of Relative Benchmarking

As much as this data can be fun and interesting, it has a lot of flaws. Although the data is broken down into six specific categories, the people in the categories can be very different.

For example, the singles could include 20 year olds just starting out as well at 50 year old singles who are more financially established. Although the average income may be $39,196 the range of income of those in the category might vary dramatically.

Another example closer to home is the category of "families with kids under 12". I have four boys under 12 but my situation is likely very different from a family with one child under two. I know my food bill alone would prevent me from living off a $77,000 family income!

Personal Benchmarking

As much as I enjoyed the quiz and the results on this site, I will always preach the importance of personal benchmarking. It doesn't matter what anyone else's finances look like. It's what your finances look like and what you choose to do about your situation. Answering the question "How am I doing financially?" is really personal.

I've seen people who make $200,000 per year of income but they spend all of it and more and thus are swimming in debt and payments. I've also met people who live within their means on $50,000 per year. Who cares if the average income is $77,000 or $100,000 per year? What matters most is your ability to work with your income and finances and work to improve it each and every year.

The best form of benchmarking is comparing your situation at two different points in time. For example, how does your financial situation look today compared to a year ago and what you would like it to look like a year from now?

How Am I Doing Financially?

If you really want to know how you are doing financially, you need to do a personal financial check-up. Start with a current assessment. If you think about it, it's no different than wanting to lose weight or improve your financial health. If you want to lose weight the first piece of data you need is your current weight. How will you know if you are going in the right direction, or how far you've progressed, if you do not have a starting weight?

When it comes to personal finance, I believe the first thing you must know is your net worth. Your net worth is simply the value of your assets minus the value of your liabilities. Once you know your net worth, your goal in the future should be to improve your net worth each and every year. Given that the formula for calculating your net worth is assets minus liabilities, then there are only two ways to increase your net worth: increase assets or decrease liabilities.

The second thing you need to know is your income and your expenses. Some call this an income statement or a cash flow statement. Your net worth statement and cash flow statement form the foundation of a financial check-up. If you want to get more detailed, you may want to look at some other aspects of personal finance such as:

- Insurance
- Investing
- Retirement planning
- Minimizing tax
- Estate planning
- Saving for kids' education

To help you with a financial check-up, you can download the Annual Financial Check Up Guide at **www.retirehappy.ca/TCOYM**

What Is Financial Planning?
by Jim Yih

Have you heard these sayings before?

- Money can't buy you happiness.
- There's a lot more to life than just money.
- Money isn't everything and can cause a lot of pain and suffering.

Despite the truth in these statements, it's also important to recognize that money is very important because it is part of everyone's life. Not only do we need money to survive, money is also important to enhance the quality of our life so we can make life more comfortable and fun.

Money Is a Tool

Money on its own is neither good nor bad. It is a tool that enables you to protect yourself and your family. Money helps you to create a life. It allows you to help others and give back to your community. It helps you to survive by putting food on the table, a roof over your head and clothes to keep you warm. Money may not be everything, but it is important. Financial planning can help you recognize that good financial routines can go a long way toward reducing your financial stress.

Financial stress is all too common in our society and we need to do something about it. The starting point is knowledge, but true success comes from action. It comes from taking control of your financial affairs and developing good financial habits.

Financial planning is a broad, generic term that can mean different things to different people. For some, it is associated with financial products like mutual funds or life insurance. For others, it's simply about getting ahead financially.

If you Google "financial planning," you will find a lot of attempts at explaining what financial planning is. Despite the fact that there is no shortage of information about what financial planning is or should be the concept is still confusing to many people.

The word 'planning' means looking into the future to make the future as predictable as possible. That's all plans are, a road map or game plan or framework for the future. Add the word 'financial' and a financial plan is simply a look into your financial future to ensure that you are implementing the right financial strategies to get ahead financially.

Maybe one of the best approaches to understanding financial planning is to define what it is not.

Financial planning is NOT:

- A two-page document you get after spending 15 minutes being told you need to save more money
- Just about buying RRSPs, mutual funds, or other investments to save money for the future
- About buying insurance policies as the solution for risk management
- Sitting with an accountant to figure out how to reduce your taxes each year

Financial success might come from a combination of all these things but it's not any of these things on their own. Financial planning is about developing and implementing good, sound, healthy financial habits for the future and creating an action plan that will allow you to achieve your financial goals.

Financial Planning Is Simple, Not Easy

Financial success is actually quite simple and you probably already know everything you need to know to make it happen:

- Pay yourself first
- Live within your means
- Spend less than you make
- Get out of debt
- Invest your money into things that appreciate as opposed to depreciate
- Pay attention to your investments

As simple as it may be, the challenge is that achieving financial success is not easy. Why? Because it takes work, effort, awareness, discipline and change. This resource is designed to help you look into your future and make you aware of some of the financial areas you can address to develop sound financial habits.

Financial Stages of Life
by Jim Yih

The only thing we know for sure about the stock markets is that they're unpredictable. We know that what goes up must come down and vice versa but accurately predicting when those highs and lows will occur is impossible. Even though we can't forecast what the markets will do, there are some timeless principles you can apply that will help you minimize your market risk as you build and maintain your wealth. These principles change as you move through each of the financial stages in life and, no matter what stage in life you are at, they're worth knowing.

Early Accumulation (20s and 30s)

Your 20s and 30s are decades of great change. Independent life is usually starting at this stage and your career is just getting under way. During this stage you might be continuing your education or starting your first full-time job. You might get married, set down roots and start a family. Your goals in these decades tend to be short term and while you know that you should start setting money away for the future, typically your youth and inexperience cause you to start material accumulation rather than building financial assets. Chances are you will buy your first home during this stage and so take on one of your biggest financial responsibilities. Budgeting needs to be a key focus at this stage in life because you will have lots of expenditures and hopefully enough income to cover those expenses without taking on debt.

Success Tips for Early Accumulators:

- Watch your debt levels
- Amortize debt for as short a time frame as possible
- Always pay off high interest debt
- Build a good credit history

- Start a regular savings habit (harness the power of dollar cost averaging)
- Get your RRSPs started
- Build an emergency fund
- Consider the benefits of a Tax Free Savings Account (TFSA)
- Make sure you have enough life insurance

Mid Accumulation (40s & 50s)

At this stage your financial plan should be in full swing and this is a good point to assess the success of your plan to date. In these decades you will be halfway through your working years and starting to plan for retirement. Make sure you know your net worth by calculating the value of your assets minus your debts; it is likely that by this stage you have built up a reasonable amount of wealth. If not, this is the time to start getting serious about retirement savings.

As you progress through this mid-accumulation phase, you will likely reach your peak in earning income. It is not uncommon to pay off your mortgage and become debt free in this stage and while tax planning is important at every stage, you are likely to become more aware of its importance as time moves on. Your focus in this stage is shifting from wealth accumulation to wealth management which makes it extremely important to have clear plans and goals in place.

Pre-Retirement (50s & 60s)

The closer you get to retirement the easier it becomes to see what your life in retirement will look like. Your financial goals and needs will change dramatically during this stage and, chances are, your experience in life has caused you to be more conservative and cautious when it comes to investing. You start shifting from thinking about growth and accumulation in your portfolio to focussing on safety and finding strategies for creating income. These are the decades when you will need to start planning for changes in cash flow and expenses and doing whatever you can to ensure that you enter retirement having little to no debt.

Retirement

That magic date has come. It is now time to retire. You have hopefully prepared yourself already and taken a serious look at retirement income planning and how best to replace your lost income from employment. Pensions, government benefits, and RRIFs become the foundation of your financial success and you must take a hard look at lifestyle and determine what you want to do with your time and money. You've worked hard to get here so you want to make sure that you reap the rewards of that hard work. Typically, at this point, you will be in the "ACTIVE" retirement stage and you will have plenty of energy and the physical ability to enjoy your newfound time freedom. Now that you're retired, it is likely that you have less income but also fewer expenses. Effective cash flow transition is really the name of the game here.

Stable Retirement (70s and beyond)

At this stage you have established steady patterns and routines in retirement. You have accomplished many things in life, checked plenty of items off your "bucket list" and those things you have not accomplished become less important. As we age, life tends to become more limited due to physical constraints. Consequently, during this stage we travel less far and less often. Assuming that your financial assets have lasted this long your focus now turns to estate preservation and estate maximization.

These are the decades when your discretionary expenses are likely to drop as you become less active but there's a good chance that your medical expenses will go up. Your friends and peers are aging too and some of your friends and associates will start dying, forcing you to think about your assets and your estate. If you haven't already, you start estate planning and reviewing your will, choice of heirs and life insurance as well as your plans for long term care. This is the stage where your housing needs may change and downsizing is a common practice.

Summary

As you go through life and walk through these different stages, it is extremely important to plan ahead. In my opinion, you always need to be thinking at least five years ahead and developing some vision for the next ten years. Far too often, people start their planning too late.

These stages are not described perfectly for everyone; the statements are generalizations and will not apply universally. The key message is to make sure you take some time to think ahead and plan before you get to these different stages in order to take a pro-active rather than a re-active approach to your finances.

7 Habits of Wealthy Canadians
by Jim Yih

Far too often we are lured by the thought that there may be a shortcut to wealth. We all dream about winning the lottery (11% of Canadians actually plan to fund their retirement with a lottery win), or investing in the next great investment, or starting a wonder business that becomes a license to print money.

One evening when I was up late I had the TV running in the background only to hear an infomercial about a stock trading system "guaranteed to make you rich". It seems as though our society is filled with schemes to help us go from rags to riches in less time than you think but if it is really so easy, why is 80% of the wealth in Canada in the hands of 20% of the people?

What are these 20% of people doing right in order to have accumulated the majority of the wealth in Canada? Numerous books and studies have tried to answer this question and it's one I've spent some time studying. The more I read, the more I notice some common behaviours that have contributed to the success of wealthy Canadians; here are seven of those habits:

1. They Save Regularly

Wealth is not built by accident and contrary to popular belief most wealth is not inherited. 80% of the wealthy are first generation and they built their wealth one step at a time. One of the key habits wealthy people possess is a systematic, disciplined savings plan. Studies suggest that wealthy Canadians save about 20% of their income. The best way for anyone to develop this habit is to start an automatic monthly savings plan where money comes off your paycheque or out of your bank account before any other expenses or deductions.

2. They Live Well Within Their Means

According to the book, "The Millionaire Next Door" by Thomas Stanley and William Danko, you may be surprised at what a wealthy person looks like. According to their research, the typical wealthy person might not be the one who drives the nice new Mercedes, lives in the biggest house or wears the top designer clothes. Rather, the millionaire next door is the person living in the same bungalow they have lived in for the past 20 years and while they may drive a nice car, it is often an older, well taken care of car with lower mileage.

3. They Know Where Their Money Is Going

Most wealthy people not only live well within their means but they also are very conscious of where they spend their money. In fact, studies suggest that about two thirds of wealthy people know exactly where they are spending their money. If you want to become wealthy, you should develop a habit of tracking where you are spending your money on a monthly basis. Budgeting can be a very intimidating word but the fact remains, it is an essential habit for wealth accumulation because it forces you to pay attention to your spending habits.

4. They Avoid Bad Debt

Wealthy Canadians make a very conscious effort to avoid, minimize and quickly pay off debts. It is so easy in our society to access debt. Every week, I get mail offering lines of credit, credit cards and access to other forms of debt: "No Money Down"; "Don't Pay for 18 Months" and "Interest Free" are all common ploys to get you to spend money you don't have. It is so enticing but, the main reason lenders are so keen to offer these types of financing is that they're immensely profitable. One of key habits to building wealth is not spending money you don't have.

They Maximize Income

A study by Statistics Canada found a strong correlation between wealth and income. The more money people make, the more likely they are to build wealth faster. While this makes intuitive sense, it may not always be easy to just go out and increase your income. That being said, it is an important habit to building wealth. Take time to train your mind to think outside the box about ways you might be able to increase your earning power. This might mean getting more education, starting a business or getting a part time job etc. No one said building wealth was easy. When it comes to achieving financial success, hard work really does pay off.

5. They Own Appreciating Assets

The majority of wealthy people own their own home. Interestingly, the value of the home might not form a significant part of a wealthy person's net worth but psychologically, owning your personal residence seems to lead to a more productive wealth mindset. Ownership gives you a better appreciation for the value of goods and encourages you to seek out other appreciating assets such as business, stocks and real estate. It also discourages you from investing large amounts of money in depreciating assets such as gadgets and vehicles. The next time you decide to put your money into something, ask yourself first if it is an appreciating asset or a depreciating asset.

6. They Get Professional Advice

Wealthy people typically have a team of professionals to help them accumulate, manage and protect their wealth. This might include accountants, lawyers and financial advisors. Studies suggest that, although they use professional advisors, wealthy people ultimately make the final decisions themselves.

If you want to become wealthy, you must seek help but ultimately retain control over key decisions.

Just as Stephen Covey feels that there are some key habits to become effective, I think there are some key habits that help people build, manage and retain wealth. Adopting the habits of other successful people can be a great strategy when it comes to building wealth. After all, if it worked for others, there's a good chance it could work for you.

Limiting Beliefs Can Limit Your Finances

by Sarah Milton

In every aspect of our lives we view each situation we encounter through the lens of our experiences, understandings and beliefs. We bring our past experiences and preconceptions to our jobs, our relationships and our families. Our finances are no different.

Money Can Be a Complicated Thing

Money can be something that excites, scares, intimidates or empowers us. Our perceptions and understanding of money start at a young age as we watch our parents handle it and are compounded by our own experiences with money as we get older. Whether we grow up with money or without it, whether money is a source of freedom or stress, every interaction and experience that we have with money and wealth as we grow up influences the subconscious beliefs that we hold about money as adults. It is these beliefs that can dramatically impact our finances, both positively and negatively, in terms of our ability to earn, hold and grow money.

As human beings we tend to devote our energy to things that interest us and give us pleasure and we tend to avoid and procrastinate when it comes to things we find challenging or don't like. If you see money as something positive; a tool that can be utilized to build a happy life and give back to your community then it makes sense that you would pay attention to it and try to accumulate it. However, if your experience of money is one that involves stress, challenge or confusion it also makes sense that you're not going to go out of your way to devote any more energy to it than you absolutely have to. It's not a coincidence that many people who aren't happy with their financial situation also hate managing their money. Whether they think that money isn't important or that only greedy people have surplus money in the bank, their negative perspective on all things financial means that they tend to focus on other, more enjoyable things and hope that their money just takes care of itself.

I Say "Money", You Say...

What are the first five words that spring to mind when you hear the word money? Often when I do this exercise during presentations almost every word that is called out by the audience is negative. I used to feel the same way. The first time I did this exercise myself, during a seminar a couple of years ago, the words I came up with included "stressful", "elusive" and "complicated". Looking back over what I'd written, it suddenly became very clear to me that my financial situation wasn't going to change unless my attitude towards money did.

The most empowering thing about this realization was the understanding that I actually had control over my situation; I could change my attitude, find reasons to get excited about money and in the process I could turn my financial future around. Rather than seeing wealth as unnecessary and a burden, I started to think of it as something that would allow me to make a real difference in the world. I started to get irritated by the amount of money I was paying to credit card companies and banks in interest and I got serious about paying off debt so I could make my money work for me instead of someone else. I've repeated the process with clients and friends and it's amazing to see what an impact a simple change of perspective can have on your financial situation.

What You Focus On Expands

Breaking through limiting beliefs takes time but the rewards of taking that time are enormous. I've discovered that the concept of "what you focus on expands" is true in every area of life and especially when it comes to finances. If you focus on all the aspects of your situation that are not what you want them to be you're paying far too much attention to the problem and not enough attention to finding a solution.

Retiring happy requires taking control of your financial future, figuring out what your stumbling blocks are and then finding a solution to overcome them. Often those stumbling blocks are rooted in a belief or understanding that just isn't true and doesn't serve us. Identifying limiting beliefs can be hard because it involves admitting that an opinion we've held for a long time might be "wrong".

At the end of the day though, it's not really about being right or wrong; it's about choosing to abandon a belief that no longer serves you in favour of one that does. By focusing on fixing the root cause rather than just a symptom of an underlying problem you can progress much more quickly towards your goal and find yourself a lot happier in the process!

Take some time to think about your response to the phrases "money is…" and "wealthy people are…" How might your beliefs be impacting the way you handle your finances? How can you use that awareness to bring about positive change and take bold steps towards achieving your financial goals?

How is Your Money Personality Impacting Your Finances?

by Sarah Milton

I love to read; I have done ever since I was a child. My mum is an avid reader and our house was always filled with books. I devour books the way that some of my friends devour movies and when I set my goals each month there are three that remain the same: 'read one fiction book', 'read one non-fiction book' and 'listen to an audiobook'. (The fiction is my escape, the non-fiction is my education and the audiobook keeps my brain busy when I'm in the car!)

Over the past few years my non-fiction choices have mostly been books about finances, the psychology of money and the habits of successful people. One of the books that has really impacted me is "Secrets of the Millionaire Mind" by T. Harv Eker. There were a number of concepts in the book that resonated with me and which have helped my clients identify, address and eliminate some of the barriers that were holding them back from financial success and building the foundation for a happy retirement. One of these was the idea that each of us has a money personality.

Money Personality

In his book, Eker's exploration of money personality is grounded in research by Olivia Mellan who suggests that, when it comes to the way we handle money, people can be divided into four distinct groups. Eker asserts that someone's money personality can have a dramatic impact on their ability to earn, hold and grow their money and that an awareness of your money personality and how it can impact your finances is the first step in creating positive change. See if you can identify which of the four personality groups you might belong to:

Spender

As the name suggests, Spenders love to spend their money. They like the immediate pleasure that comes from buying things for themselves and they can be generous to others, often picking up the tab for dinner or buying gifts "just because". Spending money makes Spenders happy but they may also have a hard time prioritizing their spending and putting money aside for savings. Spenders tend to focus on living in the moment rather than looking at the bigger financial picture and they often find themselves in debt because of their spending habits.

Saver

Savers love to hold on to their money. They tend to be very organized with their finances, often having a clear, written budget and they always know how much money is in their bank account. Savers watch their spending carefully, often to the point where they have a hard time justifying purchases that seem "frivolous" such as vacations or entertainment. Many Savers worry about their future financial security and they tend to be very conservative with where they choose to put their money. Savers often prefer the safety of a high interest savings account over investments such as mutual funds or stocks.

Avoider

Chances are that if your money personality is Avoider you stopped reading at the first mention of the word "money". If you are still reading it's probably because your Saver friend is making you! Avoiders avoid dealing with money as much as they possibly can. They never know how much is in their bank account and are often late with bill payments; not necessarily because they don't have the money but because they don't make paying bills a priority. In many cases, Avoiders consider money to be challenging and complicated and prefer to devote their energy to more interesting things. They tend to be hit with late fees and bank charges simply because they don't pay attention (Creditors love Avoiders!). You can often identify an Avoider by the pile of unopened bills and statements on their kitchen counter and the way they cross their fingers when they hand over their debit card.

Money Monk

The Money Monk feels that amassing money or giving it undue importance is wrong on a spiritual level. They don't feel right about having money when others don't and so they find ways to benefit others without building wealth for themselves. Often this means giving away as much of their money as possible, either to good causes or friends/strangers in need, and avoiding investing their money because they don't want to be perceived as "greedy". The idea of building wealth doesn't sync with their spiritual, political and human values.

When it comes to creating financial security and building wealth understanding our strengths and our areas of challenge can sometimes be the most powerful tool. The psychology of money is an area that is often overlooked when it comes to dealing with finances but factors such as your money personality can have a big impact on your ability to earn, hold and grow money. Awareness is the first step when it comes to implementing change; using this awareness to understand how an obstacle affects you and then taking action to overcome it will lead to dramatically different results.

Which money personality type best describes you? How has it impacted your financial health? How can you use this awareness and understanding to take actions that will help you build a stronger financial future?

How is Your Money Thermostat Impacting Your Finances?
by Sarah Milton

Here's another concept from T. Harv Eker's book "Secrets of the Millionaire Mind" that has sparked an "aha moment" in a number of clients and friends. It's the idea of the money 'thermostat'.

What Is Your Money Thermostat?

The money thermostat is a measure of a person's comfort level when it comes to their level of wealth. In the area of personal finance, just like in many other areas of our life, our brain is happiest when we are out of "danger" (i.e.: doing things that are familiar and have minimal potential for pain). It is this subconscious drive to protect us from potential pain and discomfort that keeps us firmly within our financial comfort zone and resists any attempts to move outside it.

Your money thermostat can be most easily seen as the amount of money that you are comfortable having in your bank account. When your balance dips below your comfort zone you'll tend to rein in your spending and find ways to build it back up to a point where you feel secure. When your balance rises above your comfort zone, for example as a result of a bonus, a tax refund, an inheritance or unexpectedly inexpensive month you'll tend to spend yourself back down to an amount you're comfortable with.

Last year I met with a client who had just come into an inheritance. A hard-working lady in her 50s, she had raised her son as a single mom and worked in a local retail store. This was a lady who had spent almost her entire working life living paycheque to paycheque. She carried no debt, always drove a used car and worked hard to make sure her bills were paid. She had minimal savings and often her bank account was down to just a few dollars the day before payday. Now here she was with almost $50,000 sitting in her chequing account and she was terrified. In the space of 10 days she'd bought a new car, given her son some money and all she wanted was for me to take the rest and tuck it away somewhere nice and safe where she wouldn't have to think about it and she could carry on as she'd always done.

Where is Your Thermostat Set?

This drive to stay in the comfort zone is the reason that many lottery winners are broke within five years and 78% of NFL players are broke within two years of retiring from the game. Coming into money doesn't make you a better money manager than you were before. In fact, the psychological stress of dealing with a bank balance that's so far removed from where their brain is comfortable often drives people to spend or give away a huge amount of their fortune, not realizing until it's too late that their wealth is disappearing.

This might seem ridiculous until you consider that our money thermostat is largely determined by our subconscious beliefs about money and wealth and our brain is driven to protect us from potentially painful situations. If you didn't grow up in a wealthy home you might believe that having a large amount of money is challenging (the responsibility of having to manage it/constant requests from friends and strangers for help); that being wealthy is a negative thing (wealthy people are arrogant/greedy/selfish) and having a lot of money might make you too "different" from family, friends and others in your social circle.

The lower your money thermostat is set, the harder it becomes to build wealth. Not only are you more vulnerable to unexpected expenses but no matter how much you earn your brain will find a way to encourage you to spend the excess in order to keep you in your comfort zone. The good news though, is that it's not that difficult to reset your thermostat. As with making any type of change the first step is awareness. Figure out where your money thermostat is set – how much money do you need to have in your bank account to feel secure? If you got an unexpected $10,000 gift tomorrow, how much would you spend and how much could you stand to leave sitting in your chequing account?

Can You Change Your Setting?

Change comes through awareness, understanding and action. Once you've figured out where your financial thermostat is set, consider how your brain's desire to protect you from the perceived "pain" of managing wealth could be limiting your ability to reach your financial goals. Once you've done that, decide on an action plan to boost your thermostat. Often challenging yourself to keep as much money in your bank account as possible by the end of the month or trying to build your savings account to a certain level is a good place to start. Be aware of how your brain will sabotage your efforts in order to keep you "safe" and then choose not to give in to a shopping splurge, a weekend away or an extra latte just because you have extra money in your bank account or more credit available than you're used to. Get excited about your money and put it to work for you.

7 Causes of Financial Stress
by Jim Yih

In the medical industry, a pandemic is described as "a widespread outbreak of an infectious disease over a wide geographical area". In the financial world, I think we have a serious pandemic that is causing people to develop serious financial problems and high stress levels. A lot of people are stressed and one of the biggest causes of that stress comes from money; so what's causing all this financial stress. Here are seven sources I see:

1. High Debt Levels

Debt levels are rising faster than both income and assets. Never has it been easier to access debt in all forms – lines of credit, mortgages, credit cards; you can now buy pretty much anything without having cash. Debt has created a lot of the economic problems we face today and was the biggest factor in the world financial crisis in 2007.

The debt problem has been fueled by consumerism and consumption. In 2005, a national Symposium in Financial Capability suggested that Canadians spend 25% more than their income. We no longer practice delayed gratification. Instead we practice delayed consequence. We have become our own worst enemies because we've been programmed to spend, even if that means spending money we don't have.

2. Low Savings Rates

The savings rate in Canada has been steadily declining since a peak in the early 1980s when it hit almost 18%. Today the savings habit is almost obsolete; with the savings rate hovering around 2% to 5%. Given that, on average, wealthy people save 20% of their income and most experts agree we should aim for a savings rate of at least 10%, this current rate is less than half of what Canadians need to save to be financially secure, both today and in retirement. This is a really serious problem because our financial future, both on a macro level and a micro level, is largely dependent on how much we save today. Unfortunately the real consequence of a low savings rate has yet to be seen but it won't be too much longer before the impact begins to be felt.

3. Stock Markets Have Destroyed Wealth

For most of the 1990s wealth was created by the stock market as we experienced one of the strongest and longest financial booms in history. Unfortunately, stock markets do not move in a straight line; they move in cycles just like anything else. For most investors, the decade from 2000 to 2010 was not very prosperous. In fact, for many, the stock market has destroyed wealth as opposed to create it due to two major bear markets in the last 10 years.

4. Real Estate Won't Be Our Financial Saviour

Not only have the stock markets contributed to the ups and downs of financial stability but so has real estate. Anyone who owned real estate in the financial boom loved their investment. It was a period of time, I call 'stupid money'. Stupid money exists when money can be made without any effort. You can sit and do nothing and make money. Real Estate booms create stupid money. The problem with every real estate boom is some people become over leveraged and over extended. When the boom stops, slows down or experiences a correction, that's when problems hit. Because real estate is largely leveraged (which means you don't pay cash but you borrow lots of money to buy real estate), the periods after booms can create massive problems like the financial crisis in the late 2000s.

5. Demographics Means More Fear

The baby boomers are a huge demographic force that has shaped social and economic patterns since the day they were born. These baby boomers are now getting serious about retirement as it is happening in the next five to 15 years. This is serious stuff because the closer you get to retirement, the more relevant money and finances become and, depending on your financial situation, the more financial stress levels can increase.

Retirement is supposed to be the best years of our lives but instead, a lack of planning, fewer pension plans, low savings rates, high debt levels and fear about the foundation of government benefits is stressing people out.

6. Financial Market Place Is Increasingly Complex

There is an overwhelming amount of information, products, choice and confusion in the financial industry. Go to any bookstore and you will find hundreds of books on money. Go to Amazon.com and search on money and you will find over 265,000 titles. Google the phrase 'personal finance' and you will find 1,020,000,000 results in 0.43 seconds. Go to YouTube and type in retirement and you will find 1,390,000 videos, including my own. There is a ridiculous amount of information on the topic and herein lies the problem: more information is not always a good thing. The challenge we all face with too much information is that there is so much conflicting information out there. Part of that confusion stems from the fact there are more opinions than facts. Anyone can now post, pin, tweet or blog about anything.

To compound the problem, we also have more financial products than ever and this greater choice has paralyzed us from making important decisions about money. Too many people have placed too much control and trust in the hands of financial advisors and stockbrokers and product sellers.

Sometimes fear and desperation drives people to take more risks. Money fraud is big business and too many people are losing too much of their hard earned money to Ponzi schemes, pyramid programs and shysters. Not only is it hard to know what information to trust but it has also become difficult to know whom to trust.

7. No Formal Education on Money

Who taught you about money? Herein lies the root of the problem. There is little formal financial education in the school system. There is very little offered in the workplace. So many people have to learn from friends or family but that creates its own set of problems because many of the people giving advice to their peers don't have the knowledge, ability or resources to teach others about money. Research has found that 42% of adult Canadians lack the basic literacy and life skills to cope with the demands of our knowledge society and economy. This is a huge problem.

There Is a Cure for Financial Stress

Financial stress is all too common in our society and we need to do something about it. The starting point is a little knowledge but true success comes from action. It comes from taking control of your financial affairs and developing good financial habits. This book is designed to help you do just that. Our hope is that we can arm you with enough knowledge to inspire you to seek out more and, in the process, take control of your money and create financial success.

The Power of Compound Interest
by Jim Yih

Compound interest is a basic but powerful money and investment concept that everyone should understand but not enough people do.

What is Compound Interest?

Albert Einstein once said that compound interest was the most powerful force of all time. He was a pretty smart guy!

Compound interest is really a math concept that shows the power of earning interest, not just on your principal (the amount you originally invested) but also on your interest. For example, if you have $1,000 and you make 5% interest, after the first year, you will have $1,050. If you let the interest compound, the second year you will no longer only be earning interest on the $1,000 principal, you will also earn interest on the $50 of interest. This means instead of making $50 in interest in year two you'll make $52.50 (because you are making 5% on $1,050 not $1,000). In other words, you made an extra $2.50 of interest in year two, compared to the previous year, bringing the total value of your investment to $1,102.50. In the third year, you will earn interest on all of that $1,102.50 bringing your total investment value to $1,157.63 and so on. The longer your timeframe, the greater the impact, which is why starting to save early is such a powerful factor in financial success.

Here are three ways that you can calculate compound interest so you can see for yourself just how powerful a concept it is:

1. Spreadsheet

The first is to use a really simple Excel spreadsheet. You can download one that I put together at **www.retirehappy.ca/TCOYM** – just plunk in your numbers and it will calculate the compounding effect of a single lump sum:

Amount invested: $1,000
Interest rate: 5%

Year	Interest	Accumulated Value
1	$50	$1,050
2	$52.50	$1,102.50
3	$55.13	$1,157.63
4	$57.88	$1,215.51
5	$60.78	$1,276.28
6	$63.81	$1,340.10
7	$67.00	$1,407.10
8	$70.36	$1,477.46
9	$73.87	$1,551.33
10	$77.57	$1,628.89
11	$81.44	$1,710.34
12	$85.52	$1,795.86
13	$89.79	$1,885.65
14	$94.28	$1,979.93
15	$99.00	$2,078.93
16	$103.95	$2,182.87
17	$109.14	$2,292.02
18	$114.60	$2,406.62
19	$120.33	$2,526.95
20	$126.35	$2,653.30
21	$132.66	$2,785.96
22	$139.30	$2,925.26
23	$146.26	$3,071.52
24	$153.58	$3,225.10
25	$161.25	$3,386.35

2. Financial Calculators

There are many different financial calculators on the web including calculators for compound interest. You can find the one that I've used to teach my kids about compound interest at: **http://www.mathsisfun.com/money/compound-interest-calculator.html**. If you are investing a series of regular investments instead of one single deposit, I use the "investment and regular deposit" calculator from Mackenzie Financial **(http://www.mackenzieinvestments.com/en/pub/tools/calculat ors/index.shtml)**

3. The Rule of 72

The Rule of 72 is an easy way to estimate the effect of compounding. Basically the rule works like this. Take the interest rate divide this number into 72. (If we were to use 5% as an example then 72 divided by 5 equals 14.4). The answer is the number of years it takes for money to double. Based on this calculation we can see that $1,000 earning an annual percentage rate (APR) of 5% will double to $2,000 in 14.4 years. The higher the interest rate, the shorter the time needed for it to double: at 6% it will only take 12 years for money to double in value. That 1% increase in interest rate cut the doubling time frame by 2.4 years!

Keys to Making Compound Interest Work for You

1. Time

Compounding is every investor's best friend because it means that the sooner you start, the sooner you can get your money working in your favour. The following amazing story illustrates very clearly why it is so important to start investing early.

Early Elizabeth is 25 and recently started her first full-time job after graduating from university. Right away, she starts investing $100/month ($1,200 per year). She continues to invest $1,200 per year for 10 years (a total of $12,000) but then she gets married and starts a family and, because she wants to stay home with the kids, she quits work and stops investing.

Elizabeth's twin brother, Late Larry took some time off to travel Europe after university. When he came back to Canada, instead of getting a job, he decided to go back to school and get another degree. He starts working at the age of 35 and also saves $100/month, putting away $1,200 per year for the next 30 years. Over that 30 years, he invests a total of $36,000 which is three times more than his sister Elizabeth.

At age 65, Elizabeth and Larry compare portfolios and Larry is shocked to see that, even though they averaged the same 8% return, he only has $141,761 compared to Elizabeth's portfolio of $182,416. Even though he invested three times the money, he has less than his sister because compounding plays such a big role in future growth. This is why starting investing sooner rather than later is so important when it comes to saving for retirement.

2. Frequency

In the example at the beginning of this chapter, I compounded the returns annually. In other words, I assumed that we would earn interest on interest yearly. If I have $1,000 earning 5% interest compounded annually, I will have $4,321.94 at the end of 30 years. If I took the same $1,000 and compounded the 5% monthly, I would have $4,467.47 at the end of 30 years. The more frequent compounding occurs the faster money makes money on money. This is especially important to understand when it comes to debt; 14.9% interest on a credit card that's compounding daily will cost you a lot more than 14.9% on a loan that's compounded annually.

Here's the growth of $1,000 at 5% after 30 years at different frequencies:

- compounded annually: $4,321.94
- compounded semi-annually: $4,399.79
- compounded quarterly: $4,440.21
- compounded monthly: $4,467.47
- compounded daily: $4,481.23
- compounded continuously: $4,481.69

3. Interest Rate

Obviously, the higher the interest rate, the faster money (or debt) grows. In the example above, if I use the same $1000 example but with a 10% interest rate instead of 5%, the difference in the results is shocking:

- compounded annually: $17,449.40
- compounded semi-annually: $18,679.18
- compounded quarterly: $19,358.15
- compounded monthly: $19,837.40
- compounded daily: $20,077.29
- compounded continuously: $20,085.54

Doubling the interest rate more than quadruples the result. That's powerful.

4. Regular Investing

The last key to making compounding work for you is to save regularly. In all the examples above, I show the compounding effect of a single deposit or investment but if you can put away money every month and be consistent about it, money grows that much faster. If you were to invest $100/month every month for 30 years, you would have $81,870 after 30 years (assuming 5% compounded annually). The easiest way to develop (and stick to) a regular savings habit is to make it automatic. That's why group retirement savings plans are such a great way to save and take advantage of compounding because the money comes right off your paycheque before it even hits your bank account

As you can see, compound interest is very powerful when you understand it. It's an old concept but such an important one to be aware of.

MONEY MANAGEMENT

"Create a definite plan for carrying out your desire and begin at once, whether you are ready or not, to put this plan into action"

NAPOLEON HILL

Money Tip: Calculate Your Net Worth

by Jim Yih

Knowing your net worth is a very important aspect of personal finance. How can you know if you are getting ahead financially if you have no way to track or measure your wealth? If you want to have a benchmark for wealth, retirement or financial fitness, make sure your starting point is your net worth.

I equate knowing your net worth for wealth management to knowing your weight for weight management. Creating a net worth statement is a basic skill you should know and practice regularly.

How to Calculate Your Net Worth

Later in the chapter, I will give you a list of tools and resources to help you figure out your net worth but all you really need is a pen and paper.

Take a piece of paper and draw a line down the middle of the page from top to bottom. On the left side of the page write down all the assets that you think contribute positively to your financial well-being (not depreciating assets). On the other side of the page, list all your debts or liabilities. At the bottom of the page, take your total assets and subtract your total liabilities and you will have your net worth.

Once you have this starting point, every year, you should redo this calculation to see if you are moving in the right direction. Understanding your net worth is the starting point to financial planning and wealth management.

Personalize Your Net Worth Statement

There is no shortage of tools and resources out there to help you figure out your worth. In my opinion, you should use the one that works best for you.

You can go to **www.retirehappy.ca/TCOYM** to download a simple net worth statement. It's not the best or the worst but it's a great starting point. There's also a link to download some excel spreadsheets. There's nothing fancy about these worksheets but that's realty the point; it doesn't have to be fancy. Incidentally, the long term tab is the spreadsheet I've been using for years. Mine is personalized for my needs and I would encourage you to do the same and take this template and personalize it to include your own assets and liabilities.

For those of you who prefer links to online calculators, here are a couple that you might find useful to start with:
http://www.canadianbusiness.com/my_money/planning/retire ment_rrsp/net_worth_calc.html

_**http://www.taxtips.ca/calculators/networth.htm**

Your Homework

If you've never tracked your net worth, now is a great time to get started. Using any of the strategies above, make it a priority to complete your net worth statement so you can set clear financial goals and keep track of your progress.

Money Tip: Know Your Spending

by Jim Yih

In the last chapter on calculating your net worth, I shared a spreadsheet that I use to track my net worth along with some other resources. In this chapter, I want to share with you another key money tip: the importance of knowing what you spend.

I've worked with a lot of people over my year career and regardless of age, sex, income, marital status I have found there is one common trait of financially successful people: they live within their means.

The foundation of living within your means is to simply know how much you spend month to month. There's a spending epidemic going on in our culture because it's now easier than ever to live beyond our means and spend more than we make. Spending and debt have really gotten out of control. This is why one of the key habits you need to adopt when taking control of your money is to live within your means.

Do You Have A Spending Problem?

How would you know if you are overspending or not if you never took any steps to track your spending in some way, shape or form?

Some people might assume this is where budgeting comes in. Not me. I don't like the word 'budgeting', just like I don't like the word 'dieting', because they both imply restriction of behaviour. I'm not suggesting that everyone needs to budget. Rather, I am suggesting that everyone needs to know how much money is spent each and every month. If you find you have a spending problem, then you need to budget your money - just like if you have an eating problem, then you have to diet.

Successful people live within their means but how can you do that if you don't know what your expenses are costing you? Take the time to figure out how much money you spend and then devote time to making tracking your spending a regular habit. I promise you it will go a long way to securing your financial future.

Do You Know How Much You're Spending?

Most people don't know how much money they spend on a monthly or yearly basis. Even people who think they know how much they spend typically underestimate.

Very few people know what they are spending but the ones that do, typically are in pretty good financial shape because of the fact that they track and understand where their money is going. They are consciously aware.

Tracking expenses takes effort, conscious awareness and ongoing work. Maybe that's why most people don't track expenses (in the same way they don't pay close attention to calories unless they want to lose weight). The trick is to keep the process as simple and effortless as possible so that you can turn it into a good life habit.

Ways to Track Your Spending

There is no shortage of ways to understand and track your spending. Here are a few suggestions to get you started:

1. Write Down Everything You Spend

Writing things down makes you more consciously aware of what you are spending and how much. It can also help you resist making spontaneous purchases.

2. Use Software

For example, Quicken is still the most well known personal finance software program. I don't use these programs so I can't really comment on their functionality but I've met many people who use and love them.

3. Use Online Tools

One of the most well-known is Mint.com which came to Canada in 2010.

4. Use a Spreadsheet

This has always been my approach and you can download the version that I use at **www.retirehappy.ca/TCOYM**. The document has multiple worksheets with other versions of spreadsheets that some of my clients and colleagues have used.

Jim's Five Cents

It doesn't really matter which approach you use to track your spending. They all work. The key is to use one and stick with it. Your goal over time is to keep track of your spending to the point where it becomes automatic or second nature. Develop this habit and you will have mastered one of the most important financial habits to create future financial success.

Simplify Your Spending
to Help You With Tracking
by Jim Yih

One of the key habits of financial success is living within your means and knowing how much you spend. This could be paycheque to paycheque, month to month, or year to year. In the last chapter, I talked about how important it is to know how much you spend and offered some different ways to track your spending:

1. Write down everything you spend
2. Use software
3. Online tools
4. Use a spreadsheet

While this may all seem so simple, why is it that so many people don't know how much they are spending and do not utilize any of these strategies? In order to implement any of these strategies, you have to have time, passion, commitment and/or a catalyst to action. That's always the toughest part . . . the doing! What you might find most interesting, is that I currently don't use any of those strategies. So what do I do to track spending?

Simplify, Simplify, Simplify

You've probably heard that the key to buying real estate, is location, location, location. In investing, may people will say the secret is diversification, diversification, diversification. For me and my life, my mantra is simplify, simplify, simplify. I try to apply this mantra to all facets of my life and it's no different when it comes to managing money.

When it comes to spending, I no longer have time to enter everything into a spreadsheet (I used to). I can't be bothered to write down everything I spend and I have never found a software program that works for me. I have four active boys so being a dad takes up a lot of my time. My business continues to grow so finding extra time is not easy to do. I'm sure many of you can also relate to being too busy; if you can, you might be happy to know there are simpler ways to track spending than using a spreadsheet or a software program.

Spend Everything on One Credit Card

When it comes to spending, my wife and I charge everything on one single credit card. This is also how we track our spending because the monthly credit card statement is the easiest tool to know how much money we've spent in any given month. Simplifying our tracking system has helped us in many ways.

For many people, spending happens in many different forms. Sometimes people pay with cash, sometimes with debit and other times with various credit cards. If you think about it, the more forms of spending someone uses, the harder it is to track spending. The only way to track spending is to aggregate spending data through a spreadsheet or software program. Unfortunately, that requires precious time and energy which may be the reason why so many people don't do it.

Not only does spending on one credit card help us to track our spending, we also benefit in a couple of other ways:

1. Spending everything on one credit card allows us to collect Air Miles and gets us a bunch of travel and merchandise rewards.

2. The other benefit of using one credit card is that our credit card has an online system (Money Logics) that breaks our spending down into different categories. (Just for interest, we use a BMO Air Miles MasterCard. I don't claim it is the best card as I have not done much analysis on which credit card or rewards system is the best.) Here's a screenshot of one of the charts that breaks down the expenses.

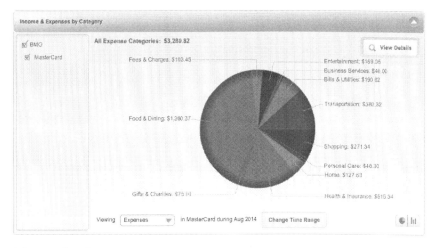

It's Not for Everyone

Using a credit card for spending works really well for us but it's not for everyone. It's important to disclose that we pay off our credit cards every month. If you don't pay off your credit cards every month, please do not use our system. It can be very dangerous if you don't have discipline or risk overspending.

Use What Works Best For You

As you can see, there are many different ways and approaches to track spending. It matters less which approach you use because they all work. The key is to find the system that works best for you and stick with it.

What Should You Do With Extra Cashflow?

by Jim Yih

Jack and Jill came to me regarding their financial situation. They have been married and working for the past three years and last year bought their first home together. They had a bunch of questions about various issues regarding taxes, insurance, retirement and investing.

One of the most interesting issues came from the fact that they had about $500 per month of excess income and were hoping to get some direction on what to do with that cashflow.

Start With the Big Picture

We did a financial plan for them to help them deal with their extra cashflow. From a retirement perspective, they needed to invest about $800 per month to achieve their retirement goals. They were already saving about $400 per month through a Group RRSP plan at work which included employer matching. With $500 per month of extra cashflow, their question was, how should they invest it?

We then discussed four options for their monthly cashflow:

1. **Pay Down the Mortgage:** Their mortgage interest rate was 4.5%. On the surface, any lump sum contributions to their mortgage principal means an interest savings of 4.5%. However, if you consider that to pay one dollar to the mortgage means that you must earn more than a dollar because of taxes, then the pre-tax benefit of putting money to the mortgage is actually a savings of 6.6%. If you could find a GIC paying 6.6%, would you buy that GIC? As you can see,

paying down debt can be a great investment.

2. **Invest Monthly into the RRSP:** The benefit of the RRSP is that Jack and Jill would get an immediate tax deduction and they get tax deferred growth inside the RRSP. If Jack and Jill put $500 into the RRSP, they will get an immediate tax savings of about 32% ($160). If we compare this to the mortgage pay down, they would be better off in the short term by buying the RRSP (32%) than paying down the mortgage (6.6%). In fact, the ideal situation is to buy the RRSP and then put the tax refund towards the mortgage.

3. **Invest Monthly into a TFSA (Tax Free Savings Account):** Up to this point, Jack and Jill have not put any money into TFSAs mostly because they did not really understand the benefits.

   Putting money into the TFSA will not give them a tax deduction like the RRSP. However, any future growth in the plan and any withdrawals from the TFSA are tax free (Remember that RRSPs are not tax free but simply provide a tax deferral). TFSAs are great for retirement savings but they are also great for all kinds of savings needs. The flexibility makes the TFSA very attractive. So which is better for Jack and Jill? Comparing the TFSA vs the RRSP is not always an easy comparison to make.

4. **Invest Monthly into Non-RRSP:** Until they have maximized the TFSA, non-RRSP savings or investing does not make a lot of sense. Also, paying down debt may be a better investment than investing into non-RRSP savings or investments.

5. **RESPs Are Not Far Away:** Jack and Jill want to start a family in the near future and may want to also put money into RESPs. Given that Jill may go on maternity leave within the next few years, the TFSA has added appeal because they can access that money before retirement with no tax if they need to. For

now, RESPs are not an option but when they become an option, the government will give them 20 cents in a grant for every dollar they contribute into the RESP (up to a maximum of $2500 per year). If you compare this 20% return to a 32% immediate return from the tax deduction from RRSP contributions, you might argue that RRSPs are better. However, it's not a perfect comparison either because the savings goal or need is very different. One (RESP) is for the child and their education while the other account (RRSP) is for the parents' retirement.

My Five Cents

I used the example of Jack and Jill to help you to understand some of the different options ahead of you for your money. It is important to keep in mind that your personal situation is likely to be very different than that of Jack and Jill.

Remember that it is not an all or none situation for these savings options. For Jack and Jill, they decided that they would contribute $200 extra to the RRSP for the long term as long as their incomes were higher than the 32% marginal tax rate. Their tax saving would be used to pay down the mortgage unless they thought the markets could produce future returns of 7% or more.

Jack and Jill really wanted to start saving to the TFSA as well so they allocated the remaining $300 per month to the TFSA. This would give them flexibility to put it to a lump sum on their mortgage, top up the RRSP or use it towards RESPs in the future.

If you need help deciding what is best for you, it may be wise to consult a financial advisor.

Setting S.M.A.R.T. Financial Goals

by Sarah Milton

When it comes to setting goals, many people use the acronym **SMART**. Experts agree that, in order to be most effective, goals should be **S**pecific, **M**easurable, **A**chievable, **R**ealistic and have a **T**imeframe attached to them. This guideline is just as effective for your financial goals as it is for general life and career goals.

Often when I sit down with clients and we look at their income and outgoings they're surprised by how much money they should have left over at the end of the month compared to how much they actually have. The trouble is that, if you don't give your money a purpose it will quite happily drift away and become a meal out... or a latte... or a round of golf... or a new pair of shoes...

Setting solid, SMART financial goals is a great way to give your money a purpose and channel it into working for you rather than the bottom line of your favourite retail store!

Specific

When setting financial goals you need to be clear about what it is that you're aiming for. Define exactly what it is that you're saving for; is it retirement, a vacation, a business venture, new house or big screen TV? Whatever your goal, be specific; for example instead of setting the goal to "pay off my credit card" you set the goal to "clear the $5,000 balance on my credit card by December 2015". Being specific about your goal allows you to devise an action plan for how you're going to achieve it; how much do you need to save and how much will you commit to meeting your goal each month? Once you are clear on your goals write them down – the often quoted Harvard/Yale goal studies are actually an urban myth but a 2008 Dominican University study conducted by Gail Matthews Ph.D. shows that people who commit their goals to paper have significantly higher rates of success than those who don't. Those with written goals who also have an action plan and an accountability partner are even more likely to succeed. Writing a goal down sends a subconscious message to your brain that you are serious about making this goal a reality; it's a commitment to taking action. Accountability keeps you on track.

Measureable

Your achievement of the goal and your progress towards it need to be measurable. How will you track your progress? How often will you "check in" to make sure that you're on track? For example: If you set a goal to pay off your $5,000 credit card debt in 12 months then you can project what your remaining balance should be every month or every three months and monitor your progress to make sure that you're on track. How you monitor your progress is up to you – some people like to use tools such as computer spreadsheets while others (like me!) prefer a piece of paper on a pin board. Whatever method you choose make sure you use it and if, after a while, you find it's not working then try other methods until you find one that works for you.

Achievable

This part is a little less relevant to financial goals than to career or life goals but it's still really important that your goal is achievable. If you're going to devote your time and energy to working towards something then it makes sense to ensure that you stand a good chance of achieving it.

Realistic

This is key. Too often, people get discouraged and don't meet the goals they set for themselves because they weren't realistic. If your goal is to buy a $2,000 big screen TV in three months and you only have $200/month to commit to your goal then you're not going to have enough to buy the TV in three months. If you find your goal isn't realistic then you need to find a way to modify it – could you commit $700/month instead of $200? Could you buy a cheaper TV? Can you extend your timeline so that you'll have the big screen TV in 10 months instead of three? Get creative but be realistic – it's in your best interests to set yourself up for success.

Timeframe

Giving your goal a timeframe makes it real. Having a deadline not only gives you something to work towards, it also gives you something to get excited about. Have you ever noticed how much more exciting a vacation becomes once your flight is booked? There's something about having a definite date that tells the brain "this is really happening" and gets you fired up and energized. Having a timeframe also keeps you accountable to your intentions and encourages you to take the steps that you need to in order to get from where you are now to where you want to go.

Finally, don't forget to Celebrate!

Depending on the goal, your timeframe may be short or, in the case of retirement, much further away. Whatever your timeframe it's vitally important to celebrate the accomplishment of every step along the way to your goal. Too often we focus on what we still have left to achieve and don't give ourselves credit for what we've already accomplished. Giving yourself a pat on the back reminds you that you're achieving something and the satisfaction of completing each step will motivate you to keep moving forward.

Having a goal-setting partner to keep you accountable can also be really useful. The goal-setting group that I'm a part of has been instrumental in helping me achieve my goals. Knowing that each month I'm going to have to share my progress and celebrate everyone else's is a great motivator when I'm feeling lazy or discouraged!

Whatever your financial goals, taking the time to define them, create an action plan for achieving them and getting excited about the life you're creating for yourself by reaching them is well worth it. You work hard for your money; it should be working hard for you!

Developing a
Money Management System
by Sarah Milton

I really don't like the word "budgeting". There's just something about it that conjures up a sense of restriction and frugality that I find really hard to get excited about and even harder to stick to. It's not that I think budgets themselves are bad, on the contrary, I think they're an integral part of financial success. It's just the word I have an issue with. I've learned over the years that often the best way to deal with something that bothers you is to undergo what my friend, Joanne refers to as an "attitude adjustment". Rather than ignore the thing, you choose instead to look at it from a new perspective; to find something positive about it and focus on that instead of the negative. It's a process that works beautifully in the workplace, the home and all kinds of difficult circumstances and it's the reason that I chose to replace the word 'budget' with the phrase 'Money Management System'.

What's in a Name?

Names and titles are very powerful. What appeals to me about the phrase Money Management System is that it implies being in control (Management) and being organized and efficient (System). For some people the idea of actively managing their money is intimidating but the fact that there's a system makes it less so. Nothing about the phrase implies austerity, restriction or limitation, just effective management and empowerment.

Getting Started

The keys to developing an effective money management system are awareness and simplicity. Firstly, you need to have a clear understanding of how much money is flowing in each month and how much is flowing out. You need to know where the incoming money is coming from and where the outgoing money is going. If your income fluctuates, for example because you are self-employed or receive bonuses, then you need to know what your average monthly income is so that you can put money aside in the more prosperous months that you can dip into during the leaner months.

Tracking your spending is an excellent way to gain a really solid understanding of how your money flows in and out. You can get a fairly clear perspective after tracking for two or three months but if you can stick to tracking your spending for a whole year you'll become more aware of any seasonal changes in your expenses. These might include increased heating costs in the winter or increased daycare expenses in the summer. Being aware of changes like this allows you to build additional savings funds into your system so that you're not caught off guard by 'unexpectedly recurring' expenses.

Give Every Dollar a Purpose

If you've read any of the posts I've written for the Retire Happy blog you'll probably have picked up on the fact that I believe very strongly in giving your money a purpose! Having a Money Management System allows you to very clearly define how your money will work for you and it also enables you to identify how much of your money is currently allocated for Needs (Groceries, Housing, Transportation and Insurance), Savings (Retirement and Long Term Saving for Spending) and Wants (everything that's not a need or a saving strategy). Finance blogger, JD Roth recommends that your net income should be split so that 50% is for Needs, 30% is for Wants and 20% is for Savings (10% to retirement and 10% for other savings goals). I've found that these percentages generally work well and, if you're looking to find ways to cut back on expenses, focussing on the items in the "Wants" category is a great place to start!

Automate and Pay Yourself First

Once you have a clear understanding of how much money is coming in and how much is going out, you have the framework for your Money Management System. If the amount coming in is greater than what's going out then decide on a purpose for the difference. Next, figure out how each expense will be paid for. Many people find that having their pay cheque deposited into one account and then transferring the money needed to pay all their bills into a second account makes it much easier to keep their bill money and their play money separate. Some people pay for all their monthly expenses using one credit card and then pay that card off in full each month when they get paid. If you choose to do this, make sure that your credit limit doesn't exceed the amount you've allocated for those bills. Banks have a wonderful habit of quietly increasing credit limits and if you don't track your expenses carefully it's easy to end up with a nasty surprise when the bill arrives. Making payments 'automatically' using either pre-authorized debit or internet banking can be very simple ways of making sure that your bills are paid on time and they're an excellent way to make sure that the money you've allocated for savings leaves your bank account on the same day you get paid. Paying yourself first is proven to make a huge difference to your financial success and is a simple way to dramatically increase your savings.

Review and Refine

Like any system, your Money Management System needs to be reviewed on a regular basis and tweaked as necessary. It's unlikely to be perfect right away but refining it is part of the process. Having a system in place allows you to take control of your money and direct how it should be spent. It gives you the ability to build wealth and the freedom to plan, not only for retirement, but also for vacations, home renovations and other large expenses. It protects you from unexpected expenses and from the late fees and damaged credit that often result from late bill payments. Most importantly, it puts your focus clearly on your money and what you focus on has a wonderful tendency to expand!

Four Disciplines to Financial Success
by Jim Yih

I've said before that the path to financial success is really simple, but it's not easy. A lot of the tasks that are needed to get ahead financially are really quite simple. Things like:

- **Saving regularly**
- **Investing in RRSPs**
- **Paying off debt**
- **Spending less than you earn**

As simple as these things are, they are not easy to do because each of them requires discipline.

Discipline vs. Conviction

Most investors think that investment success comes with conviction or intuition when really the thing that matters most is discipline.

If you wanted to become financially independent, what would you have to do? What are the important disciplines to help you get ahead financially? There are lots of theories out there including some that are wacky, wild and crazy. I personally believe that getting ahead financially is more about common sense than anything else. For me, there are four key disciplines to financial success

1. A Disciplined Savings Plan

In order to get ahead, you must put money away for the future. It requires a certain level of discipline to put away money on a regular basis. A forced saving plan is simply one where you have money debited out of your bank account each and every month. David Chilton popularized the phrase, "pay yourself first". The reality is, it matters less what you invest in and more that you maintain a discipline to put away something regularly. There are two key points to remember: 1. it's never too late to start and 2. the more you save the more choices you have for the future.

2. A Disciplined Spending Plan

In conjunction with a forced savings plan, you need to make sure that you are spending less than you earn so you do not go into huge amounts of debt just to try to save money. It all starts with that dreaded "B" word: Budgeting. Make sure you have a disciplined spending plan and a realistic idea of which expenses are important and which are not; you need to be able to differentiate properly between your needs and your wants.

3. A Disciplined Investment Allocation Plan

In the real estate business, you've probably heard the old saying "location, location, location." When it comes to building an investment portfolio, the saying should say "diversification, diversification, diversification."

The problem with this is that diversification has been treated more like an art than a science. For most people, diversification has become more about quantity than efficiency. In most cases, you can optimize a portfolio with five to 12 funds but in a recent study, the average number of mutual funds held by Canadians is somewhere between 15 and 20. The key to investing is to first have a properly allocated investment plan and then to have the discipline to stick with that plan. The most successful money managers like Warren Buffet, Sir John Templeton, and Peter Lynch are successful because they adhere to their plan with discipline.

4. Disciplined Rebalancing

According to Investopedia.com, rebalancing is simply the process of realigning the weighting of a portfolio. It's a strategy that allows investors to consistently "buy low and sell high" which is universally acknowledged as the only way to make money in investing.

Even though the concept of selling something for more than we paid for it is very logical, it is also the hardest to implement. In order to be able to consistently sell "winners" and buy "losers" we have to overcome significant psychological barriers including resisting our instincts to ditch the investments In our portfolio that are decreasing in value and buy more of the investments that are performing well. Success comes in doing the opposite and that takes discipline. If you systematically rebalance your portfolio on a regular basis, you will always sell higher and buy lower. Once you have an investment plan, rebalancing is the simplest strategy to help you to make the best long-term decisions year after year.

So there you have my four disciplines to financial success. Stay true to these disciplines and success will follow. Good luck!

INSURANCE AND PROTECTION

"To expect the unexpected shows a thoroughly modern intellect."

OSCAR WILDE

Are You Protected From Financial Disaster?

by Jim Yih

Chances are that you worked hard to build your wealth. It takes years to build wealth, and a financial disaster can destroy it all too quickly. Protecting you and your family from financial disaster can be just as important as building wealth. Here's a checklist to help you determine how much protection you really have from life's unforeseen circumstances and identify any areas where you might be vulnerable and/or need additional protection.

- ☐ Do you have an emergency fund large enough to cover three to six months worth of expenses?

- ☐ Do you have other assets and savings to draw on in the case of an emergency?

- ☐ Are you covered if you get disabled and cannot work?

- ☐ Is your family protected financially if you die?

- ☐ Are you protected financially if your spouse dies?

- ☐ Do you have adequate life insurance?

- ☐ Are your debts insured in case of death or disability?

- ☐ Are you in control of your debts? (Note: only making minimum payments doesn't count as being "in control"!)

- ☐ Do you have a plan or strategy to pay off your debts and become debt free?

- ☐ Do you have an estate plan? When did you last review it?

☐ Do you keep your financial documents in an organized fashion where others can find them in case of an emergency? Have you told someone where to find them?

☐ Do you have a will?

☐ Is your will properly updated?

☐ Have you told your executor or loved ones where they can find your will?

☐ Do you have an enduring Power of Attorney?

☐ Do you have a Personal Directive?

☐ Are all of your beneficiary designations current and up to date?

☐ Do you have adequate resources to fund medical expenses if you or a family member becomes seriously ill?

☐ Do you have resources set aside for long-term care if needed?

☐ Do you have access to a line of credit for emergencies only?

☐ Have you reviewed the downside risk in your portfolio and considered whether or not it's appropriate for your circumstances?

☐ Do you have a few safe and relatively liquid investments to draw on in case of an emergency?

If this checklist showed you that you're exposed to too much risk, now is the time to make the necessary changes to protect yourself from financial disaster.

How Much Life Insurance Do You Need?

by Jim Yih

The question of how much life insurance to carry can be a daunting one. The bottom line is that you need coverage if you have a family or others who depend on you.

I don't consider myself an expert when it comes to life insurance. That being said, I also think the process to figuring out how much insurance you need is pretty straight forward. The key question to answer is, "if something had happened to you yesterday, would your survivors be ok financially today?" Let's go through four questions from the perspective of the survivor that might help you to determine the answer to that question:

Question 1: What are Your Immediate Needs at Death?

When someone dies, there are often some immediate expenses that occur right away and which need to be covered by the survivors. Some common examples include funeral costs, legal fees and accounting fees,

One of the biggest immediate needs could be the need to pay off debt and release your family of those obligations. If you have debts (mortgage, credit cards, loans etc.) you may want to take out a life insurance policy that has a death benefit large enough to pay off all your debts when you pass away.

Another big expense that may arise upon death is the need to pay tax on the final tax return of the deceased person's estate. At death, all assets are deemed to have been 'disposed of' or sold just prior to death. This means that capital gains on rental properties, vacation properties, mutual funds or stocks could create significant tax liabilities.

Sometimes it makes sense to sell assets to pay for any tax owing but if you don't want the asset to be sold, it's important to have enough cash or liquidity in the estate to cover the tax bill and that's where life insurance can come in handy.

Question 2: Do You Have Ongoing Needs?

We've talked about immediate cash needs that can arise when a person dies but survivors may have ongoing financial needs as well. These ongoing financial needs really relate to whether or not there are people who are dependent on the deceased person's income or earning power.

The question I often pose is this: If you were to pass away, would your family (spouse or kids) suffer significantly without your income? If so, life insurance can be a cost-effective way to replace income or earning power.

The amount of life insurance a person needs in this situation is really dependent on whether they have dependents and if so, it's a matter of deciding how large a lump sum of money is needed to replace income.

For example, imagine that Sam is the primary earner in the family and he currently takes home $5,000 per month. If Sam dies, will his family continue to need $5,000 per month to live or would a smaller amount be enough? If Sam wanted to insure his earning power, he would take $60,000 ($5,000 x 12 months) and divide by 3%, 4% or 5%, depending on the interest rate he assumes that money could generate if it was conservatively invested. If Sam assumed a rate of 4%, then purchasing $1.5 million dollars of life insurance would replace his income for a long period of time without decreasing the principal. ($1,500,000 x 4% = $60,000)

You can adjust these numbers to accommodate your personal situation and beliefs. For example, if Sam only wanted to buy enough insurance to replace his income until his kids were independent and wasn't concerned about leaving the principal untouched he would just need to multiply his annual net income by the number of years until his kids reached independence. For example, If that was seven years, then he would only need $420,000 of insurance ($60,000 x 7 = $420,000).

Question 3: How Much Will You Have in Assets?

If we continue with the same example above, Sam might have money invested, which could be used to cover some or all of the needs of his survivors. There might also be other sources of income for his survivors such as:

- **Existing life insurance**
- **CPP Death Benefits**
- **Tax Free Savings Accounts**
- **Non-RRSP investments**
- **Emergency Funds**

When it comes to the RRSPs, some people debate whether these should or should not be included as assets for survivors. If you want your spouse to be able to use your RRSP savings for retirement, then you may not want to include them when you're calculating assets.

Question 4: What Ongoing Income Will You Have?

In many cases, the survivor will continue to have income or resources to draw from in the event of losing their spouse to death. For example, a surviving spouse may get survivor's Canada Pension Plan, or investment income or they may continue to work. Factoring this income into the calculation might reduce the amount of life insurance needed.

Determining the proper amount of insurance is a combination of using rules of thumb and calculations but it's also a matter of budgets. The key is to be realistic and make sure the premiums are affordable while also keep in mind that life insurance is the unselfish benefit because the premiums you pay aren't to benefit you; they're intended to provide for others.

The chart below is intended to help you visually understand the process of determining how much life insurance you might need to ensure those you love are protected in the event of your death.

IMMEDIATE NEEDS	COST
Funeral	$15,000.00
Income Tax	$50,000.00
Final Expenses	$10,000.00
Debts	$200,000.00
TOTAL IMMEDIATE NEEDS:	**$275,000.00**
ONGOING NEEDS	
Annual Household expenses	$80,000.00
Annual retirement savings	$5,000.00
TOTAL ONGOING NEEDS:	**$85,000.00**
Capitalization ($85,000 divided by an assumed 4% return)	**$2,125,000.00**
TOTAL NEEDS: ($275,000 + $2,125,000)	**$2,400,000.00**

IMMEDIATE HAVES	COST
Liquid Assets	$0.00

Life Insurance	$85,000.00
Emergency Funds	$5,000.00
Cash	$0.00
CPP Death Benefit	$2,500.00
TOTAL HAVES:	**$92,500.00**
ONGOING HAVES	
Survivor's Annual Income	$36,000.00
CPP Survivor Benefit	$6,000.00
Investment income	$0.00
Rental Income	$0.00
TOTAL ONGOING HAVES:	**$42,000.00**
Capitalization ($42,000 divided by an assumed interest rate of 4%)	$1,050,000.00
TOTAL HAVES	**$1,142,500.00**
Shortfall/Surplus (Total Haves – Total Needs)	**-$1,257,500.00**

You can also download an excel spreadsheet version of the chart online at **www.retirehappy.ca/TCOYM** and customize it as needed.

Life Insurance Riders

by Glenn Cooke

When you purchase life insurance there are a variety of options available to you. These life insurance options are known as "riders" and they serve a wide variety of purposes. Just like when you buy a new car, adding these bells and whistles can increase your purchase cost substantially without necessarily giving you a better ride. Let's review the various riders and decide if they're worth the extra money or not.

Accidental Death Rider (AD&D)

This rider allows you to purchase an additional amount of coverage that will pay out subject to accidental death but it will not provide additional benefits should you die due to medical reasons. Accidental death provides coverage at a very low cost. But here's the question we need to answer – do you really need more coverage if you die as the result of an accident instead of due to medical reasons? How we die shouldn't influence the amount of life insurance we need. If you need more life insurance, purchase it under a regular policy and, if you don't need more coverage, then save your money. The accidental death rider is an option you should pass on.

Disability Waiver of Premium (WP)

This is an interesting rider; if you purchase this it and you become disabled for longer than six months during the term of your policy the rider will kick in and cover your life insurance premiums for the balance of your disability. Making sure your bills are covered in the event of a disability is a great idea – as Forrest Gump said, "that's one less thing to worry about" but let's take a second to consider the full picture of what happens if you become disabled. Your insurance premiums are paid but how are you paying for the mortgage? The groceries? Your heating bills? The answer is that, unless you have proper disability protection, nobody is paying those bills. A proper disability plan should be enough to replace a substantial portion of your full income, not just your life insurance premiums. Essentially it becomes your paycheque if you become disabled and it should be enough to cover all your bills, including your life insurance premiums. In other words, if you have proper disability protection then you don't need the disability waiver of premium rider on your life insurance policy. So make sure you have proper disability coverage (that's extremely important!) and then take a pass on this rider.

Children's Protection Rider (CPR)

This rider covers all of your children until they are adults. Typically the premiums are small (in the range of $5/month for $10,000 of coverage) and the coverage lasts until they are adults and then is assumed to lapse. While deciding if you should cover young children with life insurance is beyond the scope of this article, if you do decide to purchase insurance on your children until they're adults, this is an extremely low cost way of doing it but it's not the only way. If you want to purchase life insurance on your children while they're at home talk to an insurance professional to determine if a Children's Protection rider is the right option for you.

Guaranteed Insurability Option (GIO)

This rider guarantees you the option of purchasing additional insurance in the future, without the need for a medical exam. This option is most commonly used by businesses that are growing because it allows a business to manage risk by guaranteeing its ability to make future insurance purchases. If you are purchasing a business policy, be sure to compare the cost of adding the rider to the cost of simply purchasing the full amount of the additional insurance today. The GIO might also be added to a child life insurance policy when you want to leave an option for the child to purchase a larger amount of insurance as an adult. Generally, term insurance for young adults is very inexpensive but this option means that even if a child develops a serious condition (such as cancer) as they are growing up and become uninsurable or if they elect to join a high risk profession (airline pilot, armed services etc.) which makes them hard to insure they can still purchase a guaranteed amount of insurance in the future.

If you are purchasing life insurance for personal reasons you can generally ignore this rider

Second Insured Rider

If you have a base policy, it can be noticeably less expensive ($60-$70/year) to add a second person to your life insurance policy than to buy a second individual policy. This is because life insurance premiums include a monthly administration fee as well as the cost of insurance. When you add a second person as a rider, the monthly administration fee is either discounted or waived, leaving just the basic insurance costs. This is a particularly effective way to add insurance for younger, female non-smokers, as their actual underlying cost of insurance is very low.

Term Riders

Rather than taking out additional coverage as a separate policy, a term life insurance rider allows you to top up your coverage for a period of time. Just like a second insured rider, adding additional term rider coverage on your life can save you the monthly administration fee and, when compared to a separate policy, this can provide some savings. Consider doing this if you need additional term coverage for a short period of time.

Which Life Insurance Options Make Sense For You?

That covers most of the common rider options available on Canadian life insurance policies today. When purchasing a life insurance policy I recommend making sure you have the proper amount of basic coverage first and foremost, and then examine your need for any additional riders and/or options.

What is Critical Illness Insurance?
by Cathy Leahy

What is Critical Illness insurance and is it something you should include as part of your financial plan?

Did you know?

- 25% of home repossessions are due to financial hardship caused by illness
- 1 in 3 people will be diagnosed with cancer
- 1 in 4 people will suffer from heart disease
- 3 people in Canada per day are diagnosed with Multiple Sclerosis
- 80,000 Canadians are diagnosed with Alzheimer's every year
- 50,000 Canadians suffer a stroke each year

When I learned about Critical Illness insurance I was surprised to find out a doctor had actually asked for this product to be developed. Heart Surgeon, Dr. Marius Barnard of South Africa, had this product developed when he recognized the financial impact his patients suffered when they survived a critical illness or heart disease.

In 1983, along with a large insurance company, Barnard helped design this product, which pays out a lump sum of money upon diagnosis of named critical illnesses. Every company, as with most insurance products has slight variations in the insurance product. The main components are that you must survive 30 days from date of diagnosis by a qualified medical professional. The policy would then payout a lump sum of money to provide for income, medical expenses, special treatments outside Canada or any other expenses you might incur. Once the lump sum benefit is paid, the premiums and the policy end.

The number of named illness has increased from a heart attack to now cover up to 25 or more critical illnesses. Some also have partial payouts for what they consider early diagnosis. This a list of some of the illnesses covered (policy wording should be reviewed to be sure how the diagnosis of each named illness is defined by the insurance company that issued the policy):

- Alzheimer's
- Aortic Surgery
- Aplastic Anemia
- Bacterial Meningitis
- Benign Brain Tumour
- Blindness
- Cancer
- Coma
- Coronary artery by-pass surgery
- Deafness
- Heart Attack
- Heart Valve Replacement
- Kidney Failure
- Loss of Independent Existence
- Loss of Limbs
- Loss of Speech
- Major Organ Failure
- Major Organ Transplant
- Motor Neuron Disease
- Multiple Sclerosis
- Occupational HIV
- Paralysis
- Parkinson's Disease
- Severe Burns
- Stroke

If you think about your family, friends, neighbours, co-workers, chances are you will know someone who has had one of these conditions affect their lives. As a result, critical illness policies are becoming a much needed and valuable component in financial plans. In recent years, I've noticed that more and more young people are suffering from these illnesses which makes it a good idea to get a policy sooner rather than later in life.

If you decide to purchase one of these policies make sure you ask your advisor or agent to review what is and is not covered with you and, if you do not understand something, be sure to ask.

Understanding Long Term Care Insurance

by Scott Wallace

As every year goes by we in North America become an older society. The Baby Boomers make up the majority of the population. Though no official definition of a Baby Boomer exists, typically the term refers to someone born between 1946 and 1965, meaning that the first of the Baby Boomers are in their late sixties right now. Many projections expect that by 2015 the population will have more people aged 65 and older than aged 15 and under. Not only will we have more seniors than ever before but our population is also living longer than ever before.

Longevity Impacts Our Retirement

Greater longevity means we require retirement income for much longer because, not only are we living longer, more active lives, but our great healthcare system and thriving pharmaceutical industry means that we are also able to live longer with illnesses than previous generations. In the past, older people got sick and died; now we get sick and live. This increased survival rate can have a very negative impact on your retirement portfolio because increased income demands due to health issues can dramatically decrease how long your money will last.

Baby Boomers are seeing first-hand how living with illness can affect retirement portfolios as they watch their parents living with illnesses such as cancer, Alzheimer's etc. and they see the drain on their retirement income. Some parents of the Boomers are moving into the homes of their children to save money and increasingly often, those same children are becoming the primary caregivers for their parents which creates an entirely separate set of issues and challenges.

How Do You Protect Your Income In Retirement From Illness?

One solution to this problem is Long Term Care Insurance. Personally owned Long Term Care (LTC) insurance has been around in Canada for several years now. Simply put, LTC will pay the insured a weekly or monthly income if they are no longer capable of independently carrying out two of the six Activities of Daily Living (ADL). These are generally considered to be: Bathing, Dressing, Transferring, Toileting, Continence and Feeding.

Long Term Care insurance plans provide income that enables the insured to either stay at home and hire private care to come to their house or to pay some or all of the costs associated with living in a Long Term Care facility. Care facility costs in Alberta can range from $1,400 to more than $1,800 per month depending on what type of accommodation one chooses. Without LTC coverage, that $16,800 to $21,600 annual cost has to be paid out of someone's retirement income. This often leads to a significant decrease in lifestyle and/or a rapid decrease in the amount of retirement money someone has saved.

Shop Wisely and Do Your Research

A personally owned long term care insurance plan can go a long way towards protecting money saved for retirement as well as selecting the type of care one will receive. In Canada today there are many types of plans provided by many companies. It is important to compare definitions of when the benefits are paid, guarantees on the premiums one pays for the plan, payment options, duration of payments as well as benefit types (comprehensive or facility). Comprehensive typically means the benefit is paid no matter where the insured is living and Facility means the benefit is paid if the insured is receiving care in a Long Term Care facility.

As mentioned before, we are not only living longer, we are living longer with illness. Protection of our hard earned savings is important to our retirement lifestyle. For many, retirement could be as long as or longer than the number of years that they worked. We must ensure that we don't run out of money before we reach the end of our retirement. Long Term Care insurance can help prevent our retirement savings being drained by the costs of care in our later years.

What Is The Best Type of Life Insurance?

by Jim Yih

If you're not familiar with life insurance, it can seem like a different language. You'll hear terms like whole life, universal life, critical illness, term insurance, and temporary and permanent needs. Understanding a bit about insurance can help you make an informed decision about the coverage that's right for you, your family or your business.

Basically, there are two main types of life insurance: one to meet your temporary needs and insurance to meet your permanent needs. Here's some key information about choosing the best type of life insurance:

Choosing the Right Policy

Choosing the right policy can be a confusing process. Some questions you should ask yourself are:

- Will the policy meet my current needs?
- Will the policy provide the flexibility to meet my future needs?
- What does the policy cost—both current and expected lifetime costs?
- Is the provider established and financially strong?
- Will the company back its guarantees?

Term Life Insurance

If you're looking for basic insurance coverage for a specific period of time, term insurance is a good place to start. It's a cost-effective and simple plan, with some flexibility to adapt to your long-term goals.

Over time, your needs may change. Term life insurance can evolve with your needs by providing options to extend your coverage period or even to transfer to a permanent life insurance solution.

One of the key benefits of term insurance is that it is cost-effective for a short period of time. You are only paying for basic death benefit coverage so your insurance costs are minimized for the length of the term. Term coverage is available for five years, 10 years, 15 years, 20 years or to age 100. Premiums stay the same for the term but increase once the term is being renewed.

For example, say I buy 10-year term insurance (T10); I will have the same premium over the 10 year period. After 10 years, I will expect to pay a higher premium for the next 10-year term. Depending on your policy and age at the end of your chosen term, you can renew your policy for another term, or convert it to a permanent life insurance solution.

There are two potential problems with term insurance. Firstly, term insurance gets more expensive the older you get. Often this makes term insurance cost prohibitive at some point in time in the future. Secondly, term insurance will eventually run out. In fact, you may wind up paying for premiums and never collecting a benefit of any kind.

On the next page, you will find a sample of what it will cost per year for $250,000 insurance coverage for a 10-year term based on 2014 data. (Thanks to life insurance expert, Jeff Burchill for providing this data):

Age	Male	Female
20	$222.50	$167.50
30	$212.5	$165.00
40	$255.00	$205.00
50	$485.00	$367.50
60	$1,345.00	$947.50
70	$4,347.50	$3,122.00

Note: Rates are higher for smokers. Sometimes you can find better rates for 'better than average' lab results.

Permanent Life Insurance

Permanent insurance solutions allow you to insure against the unexpected while increasing the value of your investment over time. Plans can also be flexible. You can also select a plan that gradually minimizes insurance coverage so you can maximize your policy's investment potential. There are three kinds of permanent insurance:

1. **Term to 100 (T100):** Some people may classify this as a type of term insurance but the reason I classify this as permanent coverage is because you can never outlive the benefit. T100 is the most basic form of permanent coverage.

2. **Whole Life Insurance:** Premiums remain fixed as long as the policy is in place. As long as the premiums are paid, the policy remains in effect. As the premiums continue to be paid, the policy builds up a cash value and also dividends. These dividends can be used to lower premiums, purchase

more insurance or pay for term insurance. Whole life requires little to no management.

3. **Universal Life:** The policyholder has more control over how the policy is structured. Policyholders are given more options to choose the type of insurance and investment options. This is the most flexible type of contract but with flexibility comes ongoing decision making.

Permanent insurance is more expensive and more complex than your basic term policies. Many financial gurus speak the benefits of "buy term and invest the difference" but remember that everyone has a unique situation and there are many instances where permanent insurance may make the most sense.

Jim's Five Cents

I believe both types of life insurance have a place which is why they both exist. Personally, I own all three types: Term, whole-life and universal life and my favourite policy today is the whole-life policy I bought 23 years ago when I first bought life insurance. In fact, I wish I had a few more "'0s" on that policy. That being said, remember everyone's needs are different. To help you sort through your options and choose the best type of life insurance, you may want to speak with a professional financial advisor. He or she will have the expertise to help you choose the products and company that best meets your needs.

Do You Need Life Insurance?

by Jim Yih

I recently read a discussion forum about life insurance. In this forum, there were some incredibly intelligent people who ranged from financial advisors to fee-for-service advisors, life insurance agents and even do-it-yourselfers and each of them had very definite opinions.

Life insurance has forever been a controversial topic of discussion. The roots of negativity stem from the stereotype of the plaid suited salesman, who goes from door to door pitching the merits of life insurance. Traditionally, it was more about making the sale than incorporating life insurance into a complete financial plan.

While some of these 'salespersons' might still exist, they may not be as transparent. The life insurance agent today can often hide behind a financial planner title or a financial planning designation.

Critics of life insurance also question the commissions that these agents make. In many cases, life insurance can pay significant commissions and bonuses although, to be fair, there are some life insurance products that pay more commissions than others. The hope is that there are many good life insurance agents in addition to the bad ones who will help you determine which insurance product and how much coverage is right for your particular situation.

No matter how you look at it, life insurance is an important part of the overall financial plan and should be viewed as one of the many financial tools in the toolbox. Good life insurance agents are typically professionals who incorporate total financial planning and can help you determine how much and what type of insurance coverage is right for you.

How Do You Find A Good Life Insurance Agent?

There are some key things to consider when choosing a life insurance agent. The first thing you want to know is how long they have been in the business. While years of experience do not guarantee success, remember that 75% of life insurance agents do not make it past 12 months in the business. Next, you should know if your life insurance agent can provide a range of products from a range of companies. No single company has the corner on the best products all the time, so it is important to shop around or find someone who can do it for you. Finally, watch for the CLU designation (Chartered Life Underwriter). This designation signifies a financial planner with advanced knowledge in life and health insurance.

Start With The Basics

The biggest problem with life insurance is that it involves emotion in the decision making process. Yet, good financial decisions are founded on logical processes and good research.

Start with the golden rule of life insurance "Only buy insurance if you need it." There may be many reasons why you might need life insurance. The reasons may not be completely logical. Life insurance is what I term the unselfish benefit because those who purchase life insurance are not usually the ones who reap the true rewards of the product.

Some of the reasons you might buy life insurance are to pay off debts, replace income, cover funeral expenses, provide a legacy, donate assets to a charity, or cover a final tax bill on the estate. The most obvious need comes if you have dependents who rely on your current income.

Buy Term, Invest the Difference

Just like in investing, rules of thumb work many times but they do not work all the time. While I do believe that buying low cost term insurance is a very smart strategy, it may not be the best solution for everyone all the time.

It all depends on a person's Needs, Wants, Goals and Means. Once those are established it is possible for an agent to determine what kind of Insurance that person should buy. Life Insurance is not a "One-Size-Fits-All" solution. Too many people make general assumptions and apply rules of thumb based on those assumptions.

The Bottom Line

Just like any purchase, there will be many issues that will impact the final decisions. I feel it is more important to define the right amount of insurance before you get into the discussion of what type of life insurance you should purchase.

How Much Do You Know About Disability Insurance?

by Peter Merrick

When people are asked, "What is your most valuable asset?" the usual responses are their homes, cars or investment portfolios. Usually, most people don't think of what it is that allows them to buy and maintain these material things and to pay for food, utilities, the mortgage and other living expenses.

The answer to the question is simple; our most valuable asset is our ability to earn an income. Our personal income allows us to repay debts, accumulate wealth and develop a lifestyle for our families and ourselves. Unless we are independently wealthy and we do not need to work, disability insurance is an essential part of risk management. Even though it should be included as part of a comprehensive financial plan, most Canadians don't protect themselves against the loss of their earning power. This year 1 in 8 working Canadians will become disabled for more than three months, and half of these individuals will be disabled for more than three years.

Consider a 35-year-old lawyer earning $120,000 today, who plans to work to age 65. Using the historical average rate of inflation of four per cent for the 20th century, this lawyer will earn $5.7 million over the next 30 years. That's significant future earning potential that should be protected in the event of a disability.

A disability insurance policy is a contract between the insured (you) and an insurance company. The monthly income benefits that you buy will only be paid to you based upon the definitions and wording in your contract.

The most important definition in the disability contract is the definition of "disability." This definition is the heart of your plan. If, as a reasonable person, you cannot easily understand the definition of disability and how/when your disability income will be paid out, then you should ask your insurance agent to explain it to you before you purchase the plan. If the definition appears unclear, be aware that an insurance company at the time of claim has the power to define what constitutes a disability through its own interpretation so it's in your best interests to make sure you understand your policy.

Own Occupation

"Own Occupation" is the most clearly defined coverage and the most expensive to buy. It is usually sold as a rider to the regular coverage of a disability policy. Owning a policy with the own occupation definition pays you an income when you are disabled and not able to perform the duties of your chosen occupation. You would be eligible to collect full disability benefits, for example, when you are no longer able to work as a lawyer, even if you decided to work in another occupation, such as a cashier at a fast food restaurant, earning less, the same or more money than you did when you were a practising lawyer.

Regular Occupation

Regular Occupation is the most common coverage found in privately purchased disability policies today in Canada. You will be paid a benefit when you can no longer work in your chosen profession because of disability or sickness and do not have employment at all. If you choose to work in another profession, the definition of your occupation then changes to that of your new work situation. So if you were a lawyer and can no longer do this type of work but choose to be employed as a cashier at a fast food restaurant, the definition of your regular occupation changes to that of cashier and the insurance policy will no longer pay you a disability income.

Any Occupation

This definition is found in most group and employer-sponsored disability policies and is the most misunderstood. This definition gives the insurance company the most leeway to interpret what constitutes a disability and to determine what the insured can or cannot do to earn a living. With the 'any occupation' definition you will only receive a disability income from the insurance company provided you could not work at all in a job that you are "reasonably suited to do by your education, training or experience." and which pays at least 65% of your previous salary.

This means that if you were a lawyer and can no longer complete your normal work duties, the insurance company will have the power to make the determination if your education, training or experience qualifies you for any other role that would pay you at least 65% of your previous salary. Even if you choose not to work in one of these roles, if the insurance company determines that you are qualified to do so, it can legally deny your disability claim.

Benefit Term

Many people have a difficult time deciding how long a benefit period they should buy. The average length of disability is about three years and your options for a disability policy benefit period range from two years to five years, or to age 65.

If you are a young professional and do not have considerable financial assets, a benefit period to age 65 is highly recommended.

Consumer Price Indexing

It is very important to consider purchasing a Consumer Price Indexing rider/coverage when buying a disability policy.
An inflation rate of four per cent per year means that $1 today will have the buying power of $0.50 within 18 years. A cost-of living adjustment rider is designed to help you keep pace with inflation after your disability has lasted for more than a year by increasing your payments each year to keep pace with inflation.

Future Insurability

This optional rider is designed to protect your future income. This rider is a must for young professionals. It offers the ability to increase your disability coverage, regardless of your health, as your income rises. With the earlier example of our 35-yearold lawyer earning $120,000 today, if his income only increased with inflation, he would have an annual income of $177,000 ten years from now.

By purchasing this option with his original disability policy this lawyer would be able to buy additional coverage without any additional medical underwriting requirements. In essence, if he was diagnosed with a heart condition, as long as he had future insurability on his policy he could buy more coverage and have no fear of being declined by the insurance company

MORE PROTECTION

"Someone is sitting in the shade today because someone planted a tree a long time ago."

WARREN BUFFET

Do You Have a Will?

by Jim Yih

In a study by Leger Marketing, only 49% of Canadians have a will. This means that the other 51% of Canadians would die intestate. What does this mean? Essentially, it means that the Intestate Succession Act governs your estate. This Act has a very limited scope of action, and its standard provisions may be unacceptable for your personal needs and peace of mind. This may cause potential problems and is very risky for the loved ones you leave behind. Plus, there is no executor appointed, which leads to costs, delays, and frustration. Intestate means that:

- You can't choose who your beneficiaries will be;
- You can't choose who will administer your estate;
- You can't plan your estate to minimize taxes;
- You can't choose a guardian for your children.

So the question remains, do you have a will? If not, why?

As a financial planner, I know that the will is a very important document in retirement and estate planning.

What is a Will?

According to estate planning expert, Avideh Musgrave, "A will transfers your assets to your beneficiaries after you pass away. It gives you control over the assets that form your estate. Only a will allows you to specify where your estate goes after you pass away."

When is the Best Time to Get a Will?

In the same information by Leger Marketing, it was found that the older you get, the more likely you are to have a will. In fact, 91% of Canadians over the age of 65 have a will. If you are under the age of 45, there is a less than 20% chance that you have a will.

There Is No Better Time Than Now

Musgrave talks about some significant events that can trigger motivation to think about getting a will, "Consider will planning when you acquire a significant asset (like a house); when you get married, remarried or even enter into a common-law relationship; when you have children; when you separate or divorce. All of these events should get you thinking about your will."

Is It Fine To Use A Legal Will Kit?

Most lawyers will obviously agree with Musgrave when she says that, "You get what you pay for". Musgrave adds, "These will kits often start with large disclaimers that state you should seek a lawyer for advice."

A will is a complex document that is worded very carefully and considers the unique circumstances of each person's estate. A properly drafted will deals with things that may not be included in a standard form will, such as tax issues, trusts, charitable giving, executor's compensation, special needs beneficiaries, Assured Income for the Severely Handicapped (AISH), second marriages, and step children and adopted children. These are issues that are not dealt with in a standard form will. Having your "final say" usually requires legal advice tailored to your situation.

What Should I Do With My Will?

You should keep your original will in a safe, waterproof, and fireproof place, preferably in a safety deposit box. You may wish to give a copy of your will to your executor, or at least inform your executor of the location of the original.

How Often Should You Review Your Will?

Change can trigger the need to review your will. Sometimes changes will occur in the life of the individual and change can happen quickly. Also, the laws governing Wills and Estates change quite frequently, and so it is also wise to have your lawyer review it every few years.

Jim's Five Cents

The will is the cornerstone of your estate plan. If you do not have a will, make sure you think about all of the consequences of dying without a will. If you need a will, make sure you seek the help of a lawyer, preferably a lawyer that specializes in the wills and estate field. I certainly believe that while not everyone needs a will, more than 49% of Canadians should have a will. Having been witness to many estates, I know that the cost of a will can be a whole lot more economical than the legal bills that can come out when someone dies and problems occur. A properly drafted will might be one of the best investments you can make.

12 Consequences if You Die Without a Will

by Jim Yih

Before you dismiss the idea that you need a will, take a moment to consider these 12 consequences of dying without one.

1. Without a will, you do not have an executor. This means that someone must be appointed to act as an administrator of your estate. This means potential delay, expense, frustration, and even financial loss.

2. There is no opportunity to select guardians for any minor children you may have. This means that the Public Guardian (the government) may be involved in your children's personal lives. Any parent knows how important it is to make sure that your children are in the hands of someone who will care about them and raise them in the way you wanted for them.

3. There is no opportunity to provide for burial preferences. In a study by Lawpro, more than half of Canadians (56%) do not have a will. Coincidentally, 60% do not have any funeral arrangements in place. Do you know what your loved ones want for their burial preferences? Do they know what you want for yours? It's a tough topic to discuss but one that needs to be addressed if you want to be sure you get it right. Beware of putting your intentions in your will without discussing them; all too often the will isn't read until after the funeral has taken place.

4. Your children may not receive the amount you wanted them to receive at an age where they are mature enough to handle it. Without a will there is no opportunity to provide a trust for your children, this means that when they reach the age of majority (which is 18 in Alberta) they will receive all of the funds regardless of whether or not you would have chosen that option for them at that point in their lives.

5. The Public Trustee is involved in the administration of your children's share if they are minors. This means the government will decide your child's financial future. The government will also take a portion of your estate, as their fee.

6. Certain assets that you may have wanted to be kept for your family's security or for investment purposes may have to be sold. Make sure the estate is properly funded. Life insurance can be a great tool to inject liquid funds into the estate.

7. In the event of a common disaster (where your whole immediate family passes away), your estate may go to a relative that you may have never spoken to, or don't even like. Instead, a will allows you to make provisions to create a legacy through charitable gifting.

8. Common law relationships or same sex relationships are not recognized under the Intestate Succession Act. This means that your significant other may not receive anything from your estate upon your death.

9. You are unable to take advantage of tax savings and save money on lawyers and court costs following your death. I'm always amazed at how little a will costs to set up in comparison to how much legal fees can cost when there are problems with an estate.

10. Do you want your estate to go to your grandchildren if their parents predecease you? Only a will can properly indicate what is to happen in the event a family member dies.

11. A family business or heirloom may not be able to stay in your family, and it may be necessary to liquidate the assets. When there is something of significant value like a business, it is especially important to plan ahead to avoid potential conflicts.

12. Ultimately, without a will, you are unable to exclude or include beneficiaries. You must depend on the law and the government to decide the economic fate of your family and loved ones.

So, here are twelve potential problems that can occur if you do not have a will. Obviously, this is not an exhaustive list. The bottom line is you can avoid a lot of these potential problems if you simply plan ahead. A will is the most critical, but often neglected, part of a sound estate plan. This is surprising when you consider that the rewards from preparing a will are many, and tremendously valuable. Hopefully, if you don't already have a will in place, this chapter will inspire you to make an appointment with a lawyer to get one drawn up.

Six Unconventional Estate Planning Tips
by Jim Yih

Far too often, going to an estate planning seminar is like watching paint dry because the information is too technical and tax driven. Earlier this year, I was part of an estate planning session that focused on more unconventional estate planning advice filled with lots of common sense. Here are some great tips I got from the speaker Doris Bonora:

1. Clarity and Communication Should be the Goal of Estate Planning: Far too often we get caught up in the legal and tax implications of estate planning. The whole purpose of an estate plan is to communicate detailed instructions so that your affairs are handled to your satisfaction in case of death or illness.

2. Planning is the Least Expensive Option: When it comes to drafting a will or other estate documents, often people get turned off by the fee that lawyers charge for their services. In my experience, paying a lawyer to draft a will, an Enduring Power of Attorney and a Personal Directives is the least expensive option. I've seen lawyers make a lot more money when people do not have a plan and they have to try to settle disputes that arise from poorly planned estates.

3. When it Comes to Personal Directives, Appoint People Who Are Health Care Advocates: A Personal Directives appoints someone to make health decisions if you are unable to make those decisions. Ideally, you want someone that is going to be your advocate and make sure you are getting good care and the right advice. You want someone who will seek more than one opinion even if it requires more effort. That's who I would want for me.

4. Have A System In The Will to Deal With Personal Assets: When it comes to financial assets, it is very easy to divide assets equally. When it comes to personal assets, dividing the grandfather clock or the diamond ring three ways typically does not work. According to Bonora, "it is usually the dividing the personal assets that creates the most trouble with families. As a result, it is important that the will provides a set of rules or a system to deal with dispersing personal assets. In this system it is also important to outline a dispute resolution process. Something as simple as, "In case of a dispute put your names in a hat and draw names." can be very useful. Making lists of personal assets can also be helpful but it is not a foolproof system because it is very likely something will be overlooked."

5. Don't Be Afraid to Use a Trust to Manage Your Estate: When dealing with younger beneficiaries or families of a second marriage, using a trust is very beneficial. Studies show that, when people inherit money, 70% of the time the inheritance is gone within three years. Trusts place stipulations on how inheritances can be used and when the money can be accessed. According to Bonora, "Although some people feel it is not appropriate to control money from the grave, it may be one of the best things you can do for the beneficiaries, especially if they are young."

6. Don't Put Funeral Directions as Part of the Will. Often people think that funeral directions should be part of a will but Bonora feels that far too often the will is read after the funeral happens. Part of this is due to our societal belief that a will should not be read until after a funeral. Since it is important to provide funeral guidance, do it in a separate document and make sure that your loved ones know where it is.

Should You Write Your Own Will?
by Jim Yih

In my Estate Planning workshops the most popular questions always centre around whether hand-written wills or wills created from those $14.95 Will Kits you can buy at the grocery store are actually valid.

Having a will is extremely important; the last thing you want is to die without a will. The laws that apply to the making of a will vary from province to province and are applied based on both the location where the will was drafted and which province the person making the will (also known as the 'testator') was living in at the time of death.

Two Kinds of Wills

Basically there are two kinds of wills; a Formal Will and a Holographic Will. Both are legal and valid.

1. Holographic Will

A Holographic Will is the classic do-it-yourself will; it is a will that is handwritten. The entire will must be in the handwriting of the testator; a typed will with testator's signature is not accepted as a legal holographic will. Alberta is one of the provinces in Canada that recognizes handwritten wills. Saskatchewan, New Brunswick, Manitoba, Ontario, Quebec and Newfoundland are the others. I find it interesting that holographic wills do not have to be witnessed.

2. Formal Will

A formal will is a will that has been typed out. This category includes wills drafted by lawyers and also wills created from the will kits that you can buy in stores. An audio recording or a video are not valid types of wills, except maybe in the movies!

In order for a will to be valid, the testator must be mentally capable and cannot be a minor. The will must be dated and signed and must also be witnessed by two people, both present at the same time, who attest that the document is the will of the testator and bears his or her signature. The witnesses to the will must be of legal age and cannot be either beneficiaries of the will or a spouse of the testator.

Do-It-Yourself Will or Hire a Lawyer?

Some people say you should never write your own Will. They are usually right. There is really only one situation where it is OK to write your will without professional help: when you have, and always will have, virtually no assets.

Hand-writing your Will, or even using a pre-printed "Will-Kit" can set the stage for a potentially expensive and problematic estate settlement. Banks, government agencies, lawyers and the courts are rightfully wary of hand-written Wills. The cost of interpreting a hand-written Will by a lawyer and a court is more expensive than paying for a properly drafted Will in the first place.

According to Marvin Toy, co-author of "Smart Tips for Estate Planning", "If you want anyone to benefit from your estate, then hiring a lawyer to write your will is money well spent. A well-written will that is customized to your circumstances is a document that will often meet your needs for many years, or even decades."

The key is to hire a qualified and experienced lawyer to help you; one who specializes in wills, trusts and estates. Marvin cautions people about hiring a lawyer who does not specialize in these fields, "Some lawyers will happily draft your will for you – right after handling your divorce, helping you buy your house, setting up your corporation, reviewing your taxes, and helping you with your car accident. These lawyers are generalists, not specialists."

Marvin also expresses the need to exercise extreme caution when it comes to using trusts, "Due to the fact that most people have very little experience with trusts, no one should ever attempt to create a trust in a Will or in a deed of trust without the help of an experienced wills, estates and trusts lawyer."

Power of Attorney Helps Others Make Financial Decisions When You Can't
by Jim Yih

Whether as a result of a terrible accident or by the grace of old age, there may come a time when you're alive but unable to manage your financial affairs. To make sure someone you trust has the ability to manage your assets, you must prepare a legal document that gives someone the power to act in your place.

Most provinces call such documents Power of Attorney or Enduring Power of Attorney. Even though the terminology may be different depending on the jurisdiction where you live, these documents are essential components to an estate plan.

What Is a Power of Attorney?

A Power of Attorney is a legal document that authorizes one person to act for another person. The person you will entrust with managing your assets is called your Attorney and a grant of Power of Attorney allows the Attorney to sign legal documents and to make contracts according to the powers granted within the Power of Attorney document. Such documents may give the power to manage your financial affairs to someone immediately or only upon your incapacity. Unless you restrict your Attorney's powers, he or she will be able to do almost anything that you can do concerning your finances.

By law, however, your Attorney cannot change your will, make a new will for you, or give a new Power of Attorney on your behalf.

Do I Have To Use A Lawyer To Prepare My Power Of Attorney?

The law does not require you to use a lawyer's services, but these documents should not be prepared on your own especially if your situation is more complicated.

Whether you use a lawyer or not, you have to be mentally competent at the time the Power of Attorney was signed. If you anticipate that someone may challenge your Power of Attorney by saying, for example, that you were not mentally capable when you signed it, it would be advisable to consult with a lawyer. You may also want to ask your doctor for a medical report confirming your capacity.

Your Power of Attorney ceases to be effective upon death, once you pass away your will comes into force.

Who Should You Make Your Attorney?

The ideal Attorney has the following characteristics:

- Has experience managing money
- Will manage your assets in a way that both protects you and your estate
- Is comfortable dealing with lawyers and accountants
- Can commit to years of managing your assets
- Has the time to pay your bills and take care of your finances
- Has the time (and the patience) to communicate with the people who take care of you

Often, the same person you name as your executor is also a good choice for your Attorney.

What Happens If There Is No Enduring Power Of Attorney?

If you do not have an Enduring Power of Attorney and you lose your mental capacity to manage your own affairs, then the Public Trustee takes over your affairs until someone else is appointed by the courts. No one, not even your spouse or a child, has the legal power to manage your affairs in the absence of an Enduring

Power of Attorney or a court order.

In this case a committee is appointed by the courts. This requires a court application setting out the circumstances of the case as well as signed affidavits obtained from two doctors that confirm mental incapacity. Such a court application is time consuming and expensive.

Can I Have More Than One Person As My Attorney?

You can name one Attorney or more than one. If you appoint more than one, you can require that they act together (jointly) or you can have them act separately as well as together (severally and jointly). If you include this phrase, either of your Attorneys will be able to act alone on your behalf. If one is away or sick, for example, the other would still be able to sign cheques and give instructions on your behalf. If you do not indicate that they can act severally, they will have to do everything together.

If there is a trust issue with regard to any one attorney, it is wise to have both attorneys acting together, that way they can keep an eye on each other and each has access to financial records to make sure that the other is acting properly. For most people this can be quite cumbersome, though, because both attorneys have to sign legal documents, cheques, etc. This could be a problem if the attorneys live in different geographic areas.

If you designate more than one Attorney, you should include some form of process for disagreement resolution and even though you have named two people, you should still take the precaution of naming an alternate Attorney, in case neither of them can act for you.

Federal Privacy Laws Have Made Power of Attorneys Especially Important

If something happens to you and you are no longer capable of making sound financial decisions, do not assume that your spouse, parents or kids will be able to make those decisions for you. Your financial information is private. Think about it; some people don't want their spouses, kids or parents to know about their financial affairs let alone make decisions for them. The Federal Privacy Act goes a long way to protect your information from getting in the hands of people you don't want having access to your private and personal information.

The best way to ensure that you get to choose the person who you will make financial decisions for you in the event that you're not able to do it for yourself is to have an enduring Power of Attorney.

A Personal Directive Gives Direction for Health Care Decisions

by Jim Yih

In the last chapter, I wrote about the importance of having a Power of Attorney in order that the people you choose can make financial decisions on your behalf if you're not able to. In this chapter, I want to address the importance of using a Personal Directive to identify who you want to make health care decisions for you if you are not capable of making those decisions yourself.

No one wants to become dependent on others, but the reality is, it will happen to a lot of us. Who decides when you should be moved into a nursing home? Who decides which nursing home you go to? Anyone who has faced these issues, either as the caregiver making the decision or the person in need of care, knows how difficult it is to make these decisions.

Often, your move into a nursing home is a decision that is made by someone else. How will that person know how to make the decision that's best for you without some direction or knowledge from you about what you want?

A Personal Directive

A Personal Directive is a written, signed, dated and witnessed document that appoints someone else to look after your personal, health matters. Financial matters are dealt with using a separate document, called a Power of Attorney (see the previous chapter).

A Personal Directive is also called a Health Care Directive or a Living Will (these terms are used in different regions to describe the same thing). With this document, you give someone the power to make health care decisions for you (regarding health care, housing, treatment etc.) when you are no longer able to do so yourself. The person you appoint is known as the Agent.

The Personal Directive only applies while you are alive and ceases to be effective upon your death.

Who Is The Ideal Person For An Agent?

Ideally, your Agent should have the following characteristics:

- Knows how you would want to be treated
- Shares your values about health care and quality-of-life
- Will be available to meet with doctors and nursing home/hospital staff
- Is comfortable dealing with doctors and other health care providers
- Can handle the emotional burden of caring for you
- Can communicate well with your other family members

It is a good idea not only to name a primary Agent but to also name an alternate Agent in your Personal Directive.

Often a person's first choice of Agent is their spouse and for an alternate, people often choose a close family member such as a parent (if not too elderly), sibling, or adult child.

Why Should I Make A Personal Directive?

The law in Alberta does not allow for another person to automatically make decisions for you – not even your spouse, adult interdependent partner or a close relative. By making a Personal Directive, you can specify the person(s) you choose to be legally entitled to make decisions on your behalf in the event that you become mentally incompetent in the future and so take greater control over your future personal matters.

A Personal Directive can also specify the types of treatment or care that you do or do not want but many professionals feel it is wiser to not specify anything because no one knows what might befall you and when, and no one can predict what health care would be appropriate at that time. The wishes that some people put into heath care directives (e.g. no heroic efforts to resuscitate) are notoriously difficult to interpret, and therefore best avoided completely.

What Happens If I Don't Make A Personal Directive?

If you do not prepare a Personal Directive that can take effect when you become mentally incapacitated, family members or other interested parties will have to make a Guardianship application under the Alberta Adult Trusteeship and Guardianship Act. This court process can be lengthy (it can take several months) and costly, can result in disagreements and bad feelings among your family members and friends, and may result in authority being given to someone whom you yourself might not have chosen.

SAVING MONEY

"First we make our habits and then our habits make us."

CHARLES C. NOBLE

Pay Yourself First to Save Money
by Jim Yih

We all know that it's important to save money: in order to get ahead, you must put money away for the future. In order to retire happy, you must save money because we know that government benefits will not be enough on their own. To protect yourself from financial disasters, you must put away money to build savings for emergencies. Each one of these examples shows why saving money is one of the most important financial habits to master.

It's Hard To Save

For most people it's hard to save money. The problem with saving money is it requires a certain level of discipline to make it happen. Most people are not natural savers. They lack what I call the savings gene. Saving money is hard because spending is more natural, a whole lot easier and way more fun. Given that most people are not natural savers, the only way to save is to create a forced discipline through a concept called Pay Yourself First.

Two Ways to "Pay Yourself First"

The best way to "pay yourself first" is to save money through a workplace savings program. Roughly 40% of all small to medium size businesses have a workplace savings program and most of these include some form of employer matching (where the employer contributes an amount equal to a percentage of each employee's contributions).

These programs are, without a doubt, the best way to save. It always shocks me when I see statistics that suggest about 15% of employees who have access to matching programs through their employer do not take advantage of the opportunity to save money automatically and, even more importantly, to get free money for doing so. In my workplace education programs, I always encourage people to save money through their programs at work and to save more than the minimum matched amount if they can.

The second way to pay yourself first is to create a forced saving plan by setting up an automatic payment from your bank account each and every month. For people who do not have a workplace savings program this is a great way to make savings automatic through using the power of pre-authorized debits.

What's Your Savings Rate?

Your savings rate is simply an expression of the percentage of gross income you put away. For example, a 10% savings rate means you are investing 10% of your gross income every year.

The savings rate in Canada has been under 5% for the past 15 years which, for most people, is not enough. Employees who are part of a Defined Benefit Pension Plan typically have the highest savings rates at 15% to 20% followed by people who have Group RRSPs and Defined Contribution Pensions who typically have savings rates of 6% to 12%. The higher your savings rate, the more likely you are to be able to retire comfortably, retire early and live a better life in retirement. It's just math. This is why it's critically important that you pay yourself first.

How much should you save? The bottom line is that it matters less how much you save or what you invest in and more that you maintain a discipline to put away something regularly. If you don't believe me, take a look at your investment statements and figure out how much of your account value is money you put in versus money from growth as a result of investing.

I don't care if you are in your 20s, 30s, 40s or 70s; I am willing to bet that 99 times out of 100, a significant amount of the money in your portfolio is money that you put in yourself. The secret to wealth is to focus first on being a good saver — you can't invest what you haven't saved.

Take Part in the Saving Challenge

My challenge to you is simple; I challenge you to start an automatic savings plan immediately either through your bank account or through your work. It matters less what you put away each month or each paycheque, what matters most is that you put <u>something</u> away. I further challenge you to keep that savings habit going for at least 21 months. Don't do it for me; do it for you!

Is Saving Money Nature or Nurture?
by Jim Yih

I have four young children and they all have their own unique personalities. Despite having the same upbringing, the same parents and the same environment, they are all unique little people.

My son Robbie, at the age of three was already hoarding coins he found in the house, in the car and out in public. Any coins he found, he put them away in his piggy bank. Even now, when Grandma gives him a ten dollar bill to buy slurpees for him and his brothers, he wants the change to put into his little bank. He has already filled 8 piggy banks with change and according to my calculations, if Robbie keeps going at this rate, he is going to wind up with $14,806,115 by the time he turns 60 years of age. Now that's impressive. Robbie is already starting to display signs of having what I call the Savings Gene.

The Savings Gene

The "savings gene" is a term I attribute to someone who demonstrates a natural ability to save. Although there may not be an actual gene that drives a person to save, there are definitely people who seem to just get the concept intuitively. You might call it the savings habit instead of the savings gene. Savers are typically people who intuitively understand the principles of thrift. They spend within their means. They spend less money than they make. Do you have the savings gene? If you do, you're in the minority!

In my experience very few people have the savings gene – that natural tendency to save. The data today clear shows that not enough Canadians are saving money. The savings rate in Canada has been under 5% for the past 15 years and there is little sign of change. Not only are people not saving money but they are going into debt because they spend more money than they make.

These stats shouldn't come as too much of a surprise since saving money doesn't come naturally to most people. Spending is more natural and definitely more fun. The problem is that spending may give you the sensation of being rich and affluent but it actually makes most people poorer. If you think about it, your spending actually makes someone else rich. The only thing that will make you rich is saving your money.

Time to Develop the Savings Gene

There is no question that some people, albeit only a few, are born with the knack to save. That being said, for those that are not born with the savings gene, the good news is that you can learn the behaviour. Steven Covey teaches that it takes 21 days to create a habit. I believe it takes 21 months to create the discipline of saving.

I think learning about money and how to save is an essential life tool. It should be something that is taught in school in addition to math and geography and history. Instead it is left to the parents. The problem with this is, if the parents don't consider themselves good savers, how are they supposed to teach their kids a concept they haven't yet grasped themselves? It's hard to teach what you don't know or understand yourself.

Good savings habits can rub off on others. I believe that Robbie's savings tendency is not 100% natural, it's partly nurtured too. In our house, we talk openly about money, the consequence of spending and the benefits of saving and we encourage the kids to ask questions. Both my wife and I are savers and I hope that our approach to money will rub off on our kids. I've seen many other successful savers raise their kids to become savers too. The really neat thing about my oldest son learning the saving habit is watching my other kids do the same just so they can be like their older brother.

Saving Is All About Discipline

The heart of being a good saver is discipline. The reality is that the only people saving money are people who either have a natural discipline to save or those who have developed a forced discipline through joining a workplace savings program. If you don't have a natural discipline to save, then you have to force that discipline by "paying yourself first" through automatic deductions from your paycheque or from your bank account. This forces you to save first before you spend what's in your account. If you try to spend first and save later, there's a really good chance you won't have anything left to save.

There's No Time Like The Present

The best time to take action is now. No matter how many reasons you can think of to delay getting started, if you know you need to start saving or if you know you need to be saving more, there will never be a better time to start than right now. The amount you save is less important than simply starting the act of saving. Once you get started and the value of your account starts to grow, you'll be surprised how motivated you become to keep saving and how creative you can get when it comes to finding ways to save more.

Principles of Saving Money
by Jim Yih

Saving money is the foundation for financial success; it is the root of what separates the rich from the poor. For most people saving money is not easy. As we have seen in the last few chapters, it is much more natural to spend money than save it. Since saving is not natural, it is a skill we must learn to develop and work at. Saving money over a lifetime requires conscious effort and continued awareness so that it becomes a habit.

Are you a spender or a saver? Whether you find saving easy or not, most of us could all use a little savings boost so here are my principles for saving money.

Know How Much You Make and How Much You Spend

The starting point for any financial goal is to understand your spending patterns. Study after study shows that wealthy people know where they spend their money and they either budget or track expenses. Just knowing how much you spend and where you spend your money sets the foundation for a sound financial plan.

Pay Yourself First

Most people spend first and try to save what little they have left over. The better strategy is to save first and then spend what you have left over. The easiest way to pay yourself first is by starting an automatic savings plan and arrange for the money to come automatically out of your bank account or off your paycheque. You will likely be surprised by how much you can save without even realizing!

Understand The Magic Of Compound Interest

Compounding has often been referred to as the eighth wonder of the world. If you really understand compounding you will understand the value of the next two principles (if you're not sure, take a look at the chapters on compound interest earlier in the book for some insights). The key to understanding the power of compound interest is realizing that once you get enough money working for you, you no longer have to work for money. It's truly amazing.

Start Saving Sooner Rather Than Later

The longer the period of time over which you save, the longer compounding has to work its magic and the more your savings will grow. One of the most common things I hear about saving is "I wish I'd started sooner." Rich or poor, it's something everyone says. This common regret is a great reason not to let anything stop you from starting a savings plan right away. Stop the procrastination. It's never too late to start and there will never be a better time to get started than right now!

Something Is Better Than Nothing

How much should you save? Any financial planner can run some numbers and tell you how much you need to save based on an assumed rate of return and some assumptions about how long you might live. Even if you don't have a financial planner, you can find all kinds of financial calculators on the internet to help you (e.g. **www.MackenzieFinancial.com**) but, as I've said before, as far as I'm concerned, the amount you save matters a lot less than simply getting a savings plan started. You've got to start the habit and you can't afford to let any hurdles get in the way of getting you started. Remember, something is better than nothing but more is better than less.

Stay Disciplined, Be Aware and Get Rich

Saving money is hard work; don't let anyone tell you otherwise. In a consumer world, it is really easy to get lured into spending your money on the next "must have" item. I've always said that saving money requires three key things: effort, awareness and discipline. If you commit energy to saving and time to keeping track of your spending there's a very good chance that you'll achieve your savings goals.

For most people, the probability of getting rich quick is low. Rather than relying on a lottery win or some other random event to create wealth, put your effort into the one strategy that is boring but has a proven track record of success. Get a savings plan in place. Often concerns about where to save money and what to invest in can deter people from getting started. Stop worrying! Get the savings habit in place and once you have money saved, then put your energy into figuring out the best way to maximize your returns.

Useful Tips to Help You
Save More Money
by Jim Yih

Canadians are having trouble saving money. The latest data from Statistics Canada suggests that the average savings rate has dropped from 16% in 1985 to 5% at the end of 2013. This is an improvement on the -0.5% rate reported in 2005 (a negative savings rate simply means that Canadians are spending more money than their current disposable income) but we still have a long way to go.

A 2006 study by Mackenzie Financial suggested that 56% of Canadians felt they were not saving enough for retirement and there's no recent data to suggest that anything has changed. In fact, if anything, the concerns are growing. Canadians have used less than 12% of the total RRSP contribution room available. A recent study by Statistics Canada suggests that the total RRSP contribution space is about $772.5 billion and only $88.9 billion of that room has been used.

If you take into account that there is more pressure on Canadians to self-fund retirement, this lack of savings is a very serious problem in our country. So how do we get people to save more money? Here are some additional tips for boosting your savings.

Only Use One Payment Method

Tracking expenses is a key part of building financial success but it can be very difficult if you are using a couple of credit cards, your debit card and cash. The key is to keep things simple and, by only using one payment method, you make it infinitely easier to track your expenses. In our household we use one credit card for all of our expenses. When the bill comes in, we know exactly how much we've spent in the month. We do this so that we can see all our transactions in one place and also so that we can collect travel points. The key with this strategy is to make sure that you pay off those credit card bills every month. If you routinely carry a balance on your credit card, **do not** use this strategy!

Stop Using Cash

Have you ever gone to the ATM machine, taken out $100 and before you know it, the $100 is spent? Spending in cash rather than using debit or credit cards is the most difficult type of spending to keep track of. Spending in cash is often a significant source of expense "leakage" – it's amazing how the cost of a chocolate bar here, a magazine there, a few drinks, a snack, parking etc. can add up. If you're going to manage your spending effectively you have to make it easy to track.

Increase Your Investment Regularly

When it costs you more money at the pump to fill up your gas tank or when the price of fruits and vegetables goes up 10% or when your utility bills increase, what do you do? Often we have no choice but to pay those bills as part of our lifestyle expenses. Each year that passes or each time you get a raise, make sure you increase the amount of money you save accordingly. If inflation rises by 3% and your expenses increase, make sure you also set aside more money to pay yourself first.

Three Key Ingredients for Creating the Perfect Savings Plan

Saving money is simple, not easy. Most of us know what we have to do but the 'doing' is the difficult part. If starting a savings plan seems difficult, first remember three key things.

First, **saving money requires effort**; it only comes naturally to a few. For most of us, unfortunately, it takes forced discipline to save but, if we can master the habit, the rewards are huge.

Secondly, **it takes conscious awareness.** If it does not come naturally, you need to find ways to constantly remind yourself to look for savings. Write little notes to yourself, or put up sticky notes in your bathroom, or schedule it into your daytimer or find a support mechanism such as a spouse or a friend.

Lastly and most importantly, **saving money requires a disciplined commitment.** It's been said that a habit takes 21 days to form. I believe that developing a solid savings habit takes 21 months. Commit to making saving a habit and, with discipline, you will be on your way to financial success.

More Tips to Help You Save Money

by Jim Yih

Given that the savings rate in Canada has been less that 5% for the past 15 years it's obvious that we need to save more. Here are three perspectives to help you save more money and spend less.

Small Things Add Up to Big Differences

David Bach, author of "The Automatic Millionaire", coined and trademarked the phrase "The Latté Factor". His theory is that we should focus on finding those small, day-to-day purchases (like lattés) that, when eliminated, can actually provide you with a significant sum of money. It really comes down to finding $5 a day that can be saved and invested instead of spent.

The point of this theory is to understand that most of us let money slip away on a regular basis without even realizing it. Perhaps we're the person who stops by Starbucks every morning for a $5.00 cup of coffee and a $2.00 muffin. Or, we might be the person who eats fast food every day, instead of bringing a bag lunch to work. Maybe our guilty pleasure is eating out for dinner on a too-regular basis because we get home too late to cook. We could be the person who buys a couple of bottles of water a day when it's free at the tap. Or the person who is paying $10/month in bank service fees when there are so many 'no fee' alternatives.

Whatever your situation, the idea of the "Latté Factor" brings attention and real meaning to the saying that small things add up to big differences over time. By identifying your own "Latté Factor" you can redirect your money so that you have more working for you and less drifting away on small purchases.

Don't Sweat the Small Stuff

At the other end of the spectrum, you might be able to build more wealth by focusing on the big ticket items instead of the little stuff. Saving $5 a day for a year will save you $1,300. However, $1,300 is a pretty small amount when you consider the two biggest expenses for Canadians – homes and cars. Living within your means when it comes to these two expenses can make a much bigger difference to your overall financial health. Buying a $20,000 used car instead of leasing a $40,000 new car, for example, translates into big yearly savings. Rethinking putting that $25,000 renovation on your line of credit could save a lot of money in interest costs. The key is to live within your means and to save ahead when it comes to buying big ticket items such as vacations, big screen TVs, appliances, and furniture, etc.

The next time you are going to spend more than $2,500 on something think hard about how that purchase might affect your financial situation. Think about how that money may be better used for RRSPs or paying down debt.

Be Aware of Your Expenses, but Focus Also on Income

The Latte Factor is all about becoming wealthy on your current income. It implies that success has less to do with income and more to do with smart lifestyle choices.

Part of financial success though, is to also focus on generating more income. I'm not talking about get rich quick schemes. Rather, I prefer to talk about the good old-fashioned approach to making more money – hard work and education. Maybe this means figuring out what it takes to get promoted or getting a part time job or starting a home based business or getting more education. There's no question that there's a correlation between wealth and income; the more money you make, the easier it should be to save - but only if you keep your spending in check.

Jim's Five Cents

Getting ahead financially requires more than simple cuts (big or small). It involves changing your attitude about money, changing your lifestyle, and living within your means. It's about living life in balance and knowing where your hard earned dollars are being spent. Every financial decision you make today affects your financial future so spend wisely and save wisely.

Do You Have The Right Bank Account?
by Jim Yih

Your bank account is the heart of your financial affairs. It's something you use every single day. Although everyone has at least one bank account, I believe most people have what I call the wrong bank account.

What Is the Right Bank Account?

In my opinion, the right bank account has two characteristics.

1. It Should Pay You Interest
Most conventional bank accounts pay little to no interest. Certainly, the majority of the chequing accounts at the five major Canadian banks pay no interest, or if you're lucky, very little. Shouldn't the ideal bank account pay you as much interest as possible?

2. It Should Not Charge High Monthly Fees
Most conventional bank accounts charge $10 to $30 a month in service fees. In some cases, banks will waive these monthly fees if you keep a high minimum balance (but they don't pay you interest on that monthly balance). Shouldn't the ideal bank account be free from monthly fees?

Where Do You Find This "Ideal" Bank Account?

Many people have asked me where to find an account with these two characteristics. Well, the ideal bank account can be found with a lot of the second-tier banks. The common name for these types of bank accounts is high-interest bank accounts. For example, I have one of these high-interest bank accounts with Manulife Bank (don't worry, I don't make money promoting them). My bank account can do everything a "traditional" bank account does; I have a debit card, a chequebook, deposit slips, statements, online access, etc. The main difference is that my bank account is earning 1.55% from the first dollar I deposit (interest rates are subject to change) and I pay no monthly service fees.

The biggest difference between Manulife and the conventional banks is that you don't see their branches on street corners. In fact, there isn't a single bricks and mortar Manulife bank in Canada. The whole idea behind these banks is to keep their administrative costs low in order to provide higher interest and lower fees, which is more favourable to you.

What About Cash?

When it comes to these high-interest bank accounts, a major concern for people is how to access cash. Here's how it works: You use ATM machines from certain other banks and pay a $1.75 transaction fee. In most cases, paying $1.75 once or twice a month is a whole lot more economical than paying $10 a month (on the low end) and if you keep any sort of balance in your account, the interest you make will more than offset the odd withdrawal here or there. Some of these high-interest accounts are part of a network where you can use select ATMs at no charge. If getting cash is important to you, you simply need to be aware of the most efficient way to withdraw money by doing a little homework.

Why Should I Change Bank Accounts?

At the end of the day, most people have a bank account that costs them money every day, regardless of whether they use it. Instead of your bank being a cost centre, it's time to look at turning your bank into a profit centre. Most people I talk to have dealt with the same bank account, paying fees and earning zero interest, for years or even decades. Complacency is probably the number one reason for keeping these costly bank accounts but today there are much better places to store your money.

Who Are The Players?

To find the high-interest bank account that is right for you, do some research. There are all kinds of different options and versions. Some of the most popular examples include President's Choice Financial, Tangerine (formerly ING Direct), and Ally Bank.

Ironically, all three of these banks are owned by the major banks. CIBC owns President's Choice Financial. Tangerine is owned by Scotiabank and Ally was bought by the RBC. As a result, the interest rate on these three high interest bank accounts have come down a bit since their independent days but they still remain a better alternative than paying fees and earning no interest.

The Bottom Line: It's up to you to make the next move

If you have not reviewed your bank account in a long time, if ever, what are you waiting for? It's time to put money in your pockets instead of adding them to the huge profits of the big banks.

TFSA vs. RRSP: The New Debate
by Jim Yih

For as long as I have been in the business, the biggest debate about RRSPs has been the debate over which is better: buying RRSPs or pay down your mortgage. There has been lots written on this topic, and several online articles that have tackled the debate including:

Debate: RRSP vs. Mortgage on **Million Dollar Journey** (www.milliondollarjourney.com)

Contribute to RRSP or Pay Down Mortgage on **Canadian Finance Blog** (www.canadianfinanceblog.com)

I even tackled this topic on www.retirehappy.ca in an article called *The Great RRSP Debate*

TFSAs Created a New Debate

A new debate began in 2008 when then Finance Minister Jim Flaherty, announced what he considered to be the historically significant introduction of Tax-Free Savings Accounts (TFSA). Tax expert Jamie Golombek brought some real attention to the debate when he suggested that more people may want to look at putting money into Tax Free Savings Accounts (TFSAs). In fact, he went so far as to suggest that, in some cases, TFSAs might even be more beneficial than RRSPs.

Just recently, I cautioned people from thinking that TFSAs are better savings vehicles than RRSPs for retirement when I shared two reasons why TFSAs will not replace the RRSP as the primary way to save for retirement: 1. It's too easy to access the money in a TFSA for something other than retirement because there's no tax consequence on withdrawals and 2. While the contribution limits are manageable they may not be enough for retirement savings.

The Ins and Outs of RRSPs and TFSAs

Let's look at some of the math used in the debate over the use of RRSPs or TFSAs for retirement savings. RRSPs are attractive because you get an immediate tax deduction for the contribution and any investment earnings are tax sheltered for as long as the money stays in the RRSP. Depending on your marginal tax rate, a $5,000 contribution might translate into tax savings of $1,250 to $2,000 as a result of the immediate tax deduction. The TFSA does not give you this tax deduction which makes the RRSP pretty appealing.

However, you can't properly compare TFSA with the RRSP by just looking at the tax savings going into the plans. You also have to look into the future when the money comes out of the plans. With the RRSP any withdrawal is fully taxable. That means a withdrawal of $5,000 might only net you $3,000 - $4,000 after tax, depending on your marginal tax rate. TFSAs may not give you a deduction when you put the money in but you also don't have to pay tax when you take the money out so if you withdraw $5,000, you get the full $5,000.

In both TFSAs and RRSPs, you get the benefit of tax sheltered growth because you don't have to pay tax on any investment earnings or growth while the investments are in the account. When you withdraw the money though, the investment growth is taxable on withdrawal from the RRSP and tax-free on withdrawal from the TFSA. This tax-free growth is what makes TFSAs so powerful.

Marginal Tax Rates Make All The Difference

If you're debating putting money into a RRSP or TFSA, take a look at your marginal tax rates. The bottom line is that RRSPs still make sense if you are saving long term for retirement and you expect your income at the time of withdrawal to be in a lower tax bracket than your income at the time of contribution into the RRSP. Here's a great rule of thumb to follow:

1. If your marginal tax rate at the time of contribution is greater than your marginal tax rate at the time of withdrawal, then RRSPs have the advantage.

2. If your marginal tax rate at the time of contribution is less than your marginal tax rate at the time of withdrawal, then TFSAs have the advantage.

3. If your marginal tax rate at the time of contribution is equal than your marginal tax rate at the time of withdrawal, then neither has the advantage.

This logic is what I call the "one formula approach" to making RRSP contribution decisions.

Jim's Five Cents

RRSPs and TFSAs both have a place for savings. If you have the money, you should do both.

If you don't have the money to do both, then start by looking at what you are saving for. If you are saving for retirement, then my advice is to start with the RRSPs and use the one formula approach above to see if the tax implications now and in retirement work in your favour. If they don't, then it might make more sense to save in the TFSA.

If you are saving to buy a car, go on a holiday or for an emergency, then the TFSA is probably the way to go because when you are saving with the intention of spending the money before retirement the fact that there is no tax when you withdraw money gives the TFSA a huge advantage.

Choosing the Right Savings Vehicle
by Jim Yih

Saving money is such a critical component of financial success. Unfortunately, Canadians have not been good savers for a long time. This is partly because saving money is a learned behaviour and few people are given the opportunity to learn it properly. You don't get much of a financial education in schools, and it's rare to find programs in the workplace. Most people are left to learn about saving money at home but unfortunately, most parents are not good savers themselves, and many never talk to their kids about money.

The key point to start with, is that saving money for your future is most effective when you have a clear idea of your goals.

Why Save Money?

The answer to this question very much depends on your goals. Some people save to spend - they are planning to buy a car, or a house, or shoes, to take a vacation, or to renovate the kitchen. Some people save for their children's education, others for retirement and, believe it or not, there are some people who are saving simply because they can't spend all their money.

The first step in saving money though, is to know what you will use the money for because this will help you determine the appropriate savings vehicle to use.

If you are saving money for your child's education for example, then a Registered Education Savings Plan (RESP) will likely be the best tool. If you're saving for a holiday, you would never use an RESP because a vehicle such as a Tax-Free Savings Account (TFSA) would be much more appropriate. Saving for retirement is probably the most complicated, because you could use a

Registered Retirement Savings Plan (RRSP), a TFSA or several other options.

Which Type of Account?

Before we go further, it's important to understand the difference between an account and an investment. This idea is often misunderstood by people who are starting their savings journey. One way to understand the difference is to think of an account as a bucket, and an investment as something you carry inside the bucket.

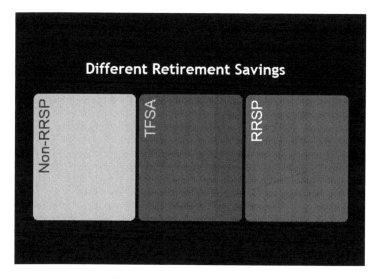

The various account "buckets" in Canada include the ones we just mentioned, the Registered Retirement Savings Plan (RRSP); Tax-Free Savings Account (TFSA); Registered Education Savings Plan (RESPs) as well as Registered Retirement Income Funds (RRIF); Locked-in Retirement Accounts (LIRA), and plain old Non-Registered (taxable) accounts. Each of these has different rules regarding the amount you can contribute, when you can withdraw the money, and how the growth and income are taxed.

An investment is a type of asset that you hold inside one of these buckets. For example, with the money in your RRSP bucket, you can buy a whole range of investments, such as mutual funds, stocks, bonds, Guaranteed Investment Certificates (GICs), exchange-traded funds (ETFs), and many others.

Let's quickly walk through the four main accounts you can use to save money:

Registered Retirement Savings Plan (RRSP)

The RRSP was created back in 1957 and is primarily used to save for retirement. The incentive to use a RRSP is really tax-driven: When you put money into an RRSP, your contribution qualifies for a tax deduction. Any investment growth is tax-deferred until withdrawal. But when you eventually take money out of your RRSP (usually in retirement), it is fully taxable. You can also make early withdrawals from RRSPs to buy your first home or to pay for your own education. Your RRSP contribution limit is determined by the amount of income you earn.

Registered Education Savings Plan (RESP)

The RESP is designed specifically to help you save for a child's education. RESPs are attractive because of the Canada Education Savings Grant: for every dollar you contribute to the RESP (to a maximum of $2,500 per child per year), the government will contribute 20 cents. As long as the money stays in the plan, there is no tax on any investment growth. Later, when the money is withdrawn to pay for your child's education, the growth is taxed in the child's hands, so there is usually little or no tax.

Tax-Free Savings Accounts (TFSA)

The TFSA is the newest type of account; it was introduced in 2009. Unlike the RRSP, there is no tax deduction for contributions but any growth on investments held inside a TFSA is tax free and can be withdrawn at any time without any tax consequences. The maximum amount you could contribute to a TFSA in 2009-2012 was $5,000/year. In 2013 the limit was raised to $5,500/year and it will no doubt be raised again in the future. This means that, in 2014, anyone who was over the age of 18 in 2009 and who has never contributed to a TFSA would have $31,500 of contribution room. If you are unsure of your personal contribution room, your most recent Notice of Assessment will tell you what it is.

One of the many powerful features of the TFSA is that, unlike the RRSP, when you withdraw money you get the contribution room back and can replace the amount you withdrew (provided you don't do this any earlier than the following calendar year.)

This rule also applies to any growth on investments held inside a TFSA. If, for example, someone had invested $31,500 inside their TFSA and the value of their investments had grown to $50,000. They could withdraw the full $50,000 in 2014 and then in 2015 they would be permitted to contribute up to $50,500 (the $50,000 they withdrew + their $5,500 contribution room for 2015).

Non-Registered Account

A non-registered account is just a general investment account. It offers no tax deduction on contributions, and all of the growth is taxable: interest income, dividends, and capital gains have different tax treatments, but the Canada Revenue Agency takes a slice of each. In most cases, you would only use a non-registered account when your TFSA contribution room is all used up.

As you can see, different accounts have different tax treatments and different rules. That also means different accounts will be more appropriate for different savings objectives. You can save money more effectively if you choose the type of account that is the best match with your savings goals.

PAY DOWN YOUR DEBTS

"You must walk to the beat of a different drummer. The same beat that the wealthy hear. If the beat sounds normal, evacuate the dance floor immediately! The goal is to not be normal, because normal is broke."

DAVE RAMSEY

Make a Debt Plan
by Sarah Milton

We live in a society where pretty much anything that we want is available to us as long as we have enough credit to pay for it and where carrying consumer debt is an accepted fact of life. Our economy depends on consumers spending money on "stuff" and our financial institutions are making massive profits from financing that spending. However, when so many people are shouldering increasingly large amounts of consumer debt, what happens when interest rates start to rise?

Many financial experts are warning that, when interest rates start to return to the levels they were at before the markets dropped in 2008, many people will find themselves struggling to make their minimum payment requirements. Debt is a burden that can consume a huge chunk of our monthly expenses and has the ability to seriously hamper our pursuit of financial success. Its impact is not just financial; it can be emotional, physical and psychological too and this is all the more reason to conquer it. It's time to develop a debt plan.

Take Stock of Your Debt Situation

The first step in conquering debt is to take an honest look at your situation so you can develop a debt plan. Make sure that you're fully aware of the amount of debt that you're carrying; make a list of who you owe, how much you owe and how much interest you're paying as well as the minimum payments required on each item. It can be incredibly scary (especially for those with an Avoider money personality) to see the reality of your situation laid out in black and white but it's important for you to know where you are so that you can put a plan in place that will not only get you out of debt but will also keep you there.

Identify Your Pitfalls

Whatever the reality of your situation is, it's highly unlikely that you got there overnight and chances are you didn't get there by accident. Life does throw financial curveballs but often our own habits make the bad luck worse. It can be really hard to acknowledge our own role in creating a less than desirable situation but if you don't take the time to consider which habits helped you dig the debt hole, you're setting yourself up to repeat them down the road. So many of us have cleared off credit card debt with a consolidation loan, only to find that by the time the loan is finally paid off we've managed to run the debt right back up again; we fixed the symptom but not the underlying cause of the problem.

Taking an honest look at our situation, understanding the spending habits that lure us into debt and the influence of psychological factors such as our money personality, financial thermostat and limiting beliefs means that we can put a plan in place to avoid repeating the same mistakes. In doing this we dramatically increase our chances of getting out of debt and staying that way.

Know Your Cash Flow

If you've read any of my posts for Retire Happy there's a good chance you'll have picked up on the fact that I'm a big fan of giving your money a purpose. Being aware of all the money flowing into your life and making sure that every dollar has a purpose is a great way of reducing the chances that your hard-earned money will drift away and become shoes or a new sweater. If you're serious about getting out of debt you have to know how much money you can commit to conquering your debt each month and what percentage of any extra money that comes in will also be committed to debt elimination. Taking some time to create a money management system will help you keep track of your spending, identify areas where you can reduce your expenses and give you a tangible way of monitoring your progress. It doesn't have to be complicated (simple is usually best) but having a system will help you enormously in getting to where you want to go and helping you stay on track.

Make a Debt Plan

There are a number of strategies for conquering debt and a number of Advisors and non-profit agencies who can help with credit counselling and budgeting. I've used Dave Ramsay's "Debt Snowball" concept with several clients and have found it to be simple and effective. All you do is arrange your debts in order from smallest to largest. You pay the minimum payment on each debt every month and then put every dollar you've committed to 'debt-busting' against the smallest debt until it's paid off in full. Then you 'snowball' the debt-busting dollars plus the amount of the minimum payment you were making on the debt that's paid off and apply the money to the second smallest debt. The more of your debts you pay off, the greater the amount of money that you're applying so by the time you get to the biggest debt you're paying off a significant chunk each month and it gets paid off sooner.

The most important thing about the plan you choose is making sure that it will get you to your goal, after that all you need to do is to commit to working it. Just because debt is a fact of life in the world we live in doesn't mean that we have to buy in to carrying it. Living debt free is a key factor in building wealth and retiring happy and the sooner we start, the happier we will be.

Stress Test Your Debt

by Jim Yih

With interest rates at 50-year lows, many people are wondering if interest rates are going to go up. Canadians who hold debt are obviously hoping that interest rates stay low but investors (especially conservative investors) are hoping that interest rates go back up to double digits so they can get better guaranteed returns.

Interestingly, that last paragraph was the first paragraph of an article I wrote for the Edmonton Journal back in 2004. As you can see, times have not changed much since then: We are still sitting in a low interest rate environment. We are still talking about the possibility or likelihood that interest rates will rise. And we still have no clue what the future will hold!

What I find interesting about the interest rate debate is the speculation for rising interest rates has been going on for over 10 years now and every time someone says "rates have to go up" or "they can't go lower" they seem to go lower.

Back in 2004 when I wrote the article, 5-year mortgage rates were about 4.9%. Today, with mortgage rates hovering around 3% and GIC rates even lower than that, it's getting easier to argue that rates are likely to go up but the next question is "How much?"

No-one really knows if rates will rise or how much they will go up but rest assured that rising interest rates will impact anyone and everyone with a mortgage or other forms of debt.

If you want to properly prepare yourself for the impact of rising interest rates, it's important to stress test your debt. Run some scenarios on your debt to see how higher interest rates will affect your payments, the time it will take you to pay off your debt and how much interest you will pay overall.

What if Interest Rates Increase?

Let's take a look at an example of stress testing your debt.

Jackson and Rebecca have a $250,000 mortgage, $12,000 owing on their MasterCard and $32,000 on their line of credit. The mortgage is currently at 2.9% and will come up for renewal in two years. Their monthly payments are $1,175 (not including property taxes). To stress test their mortgage, let's take a look at some 'what if' scenarios to see what the impact of rising interest rates might be on their debt.

Scenario 1: Interest Rates Rise 1%
In two years, they will have an outstanding balance of $235,000 on their mortgage at renewal. At 3.9% with the same remaining amortization, their monthly mortgage payment will go up to $1,363.51 per month. That's an increased monthly payment of $188.51 and the total cost of interest over the amortization period would increase from $75,535.45 to $108,603.61. That's significant!

Scenario 2: Interest Rates Rise 1.5%
At 4.4%, payments will rise $250 per month to $1,425 per month.

Scenario 3: Interest Rates Rise 2%
At 4.9%, their payments will rise $313 per month to $1,488 per month. Total interest paid over the amortization period would almost double to $140,103.11.

Note: The last time 5-year mortgage rates were over 4.5% was May 2010. The last time 5-year mortgage rates were over 5% was January 2009.

Jim's Five Cents

So what's the point? I'm not here to try and predict where interest rates are going or how much they will increase in two years. The truth is I have no clue. The point I am trying to make is that the possibility of mortgage rates being 4%, 5% or more is real. If interest rates rise, will you be in a position to be able to handle higher payments? What will be the longer-term impact of that rise on your total interest costs?

Financial planning is about looking into the future in an effort to make that future less unpredictable. Jackson and Rebecca felt they could handle increased mortgage payments of $200 to $250 per month but what about the impact of higher interest rates on their credit cards and the line of credit? When it comes to stress testing your debt, you have to stress test all forms of debt.

Here's one final thought for Jackson and Rebecca: If they can afford an extra $200 per month increase in their mortgage payment, why wouldn't they put that against the mortgage now? Increasing payments in a low interest rate environment means they could pay their debt off faster and it will give them more flexibility and more options when interest rates rise in the future.

5 Ways to Pay Off Your Credit Cards

by Jim Yih

It seems as though, after every Christmas season has come and gone, many of us find ourselves nervously anticipating the upcoming credit card statements and trying to figure how best to pay off the debt. The worst thing you can do financially is carry credit card debt. This is not only because credit and store cards tend to have the highest interest rates (up to 29.9%) but also because that interest is compounded daily which means it increases much faster than interest on a loan or line of credit. Christmas is fun because it is the season for giving but, if the bills are still there long after the thrill of giving and receiving has gone, that takes a lot of the fun out of the giving experience.

In today's world almost everyone uses credit but most people get little to no training on using credit wisely. If you're currently carrying a balance on your credit card, here are some strategies to help you get out of credit card debt:

1. Pay More Than The Minimum: Most credit cards require a minimum payment of 3% of the outstanding balance. Paying the minimum only prolongs the agony. Quite frankly that's exactly what the banks want you to do. If you carry a $1,000 balance on your credit card at 28.8% interest, your minimum payment is $30 per month and a significant percentage of that minimum payment is interest. At that rate, it would take you 68 months (over 5 years) to pay off that $1,000 balance and you would pay about $1,040 of interest on a $1,000 debt. That's crazy! If you double up the minimum payment to $60 per month, your additional $30 goes straight towards the principal which means you'll have the debt paid off in only 22 months and your total interest would be less than $300. That's over $700 of interest saved on a $1,000 credit card debt! Always pay off as much of your credit card balance as you can, or best yet, pay it off every month.

2. Consolidate Your Debt to a Lower Interest Rate: According to Tricia French, Financial Counsellor for SISIP Financial Services, "There are really only two ways to get out of debt; pay it down as fast as you can or find credit at the lowest interest rate." One of the ways to get a lower interest rate is to consolidate your debt at a lower rate.

The best option if you have good credit is to consolidate the debt using a line of credit because it usually has the lowest interest rate. Someone with $10,000 of credit card debt from various credit cards paying an average of 15% in interest would have a minimum monthly payment on that debt of $300 per month. Of that $300 payment, $125 would go to interest and $175 would go to principal. If they consolidated that debt into a line of credit at 8% and continued to pay the same $300 per month in payments, the interest portion would only be $67 per month which means $233 would go towards principal and the debt would be paid off a lot sooner.

3. Pay The Highest Interest First: For some people, debt has become so overwhelming that consolidation is not an option. In that case, it's time to get really serious and start attacking the highest interest debt first. The math on this strategy is really simple; higher interest rates mean more money in the banks' pockets. Pay high interest debt off first. Once a card is paid off, don't run it up again. A credit card with a zero balance can often be a temptation to spend. To avoid the urge, stash it away, lower your credit limit or better yet, cut up the card.

4. Switch to Low Interest Rate Credit Cards: If you are carrying a balance on your card of more than $1,000 it makes sense to ask your lender about switching to their low rate card. Despite the annual fee, you will save interest and speed up your repayment. If you plan to pay your balance in full each month once you've got your card paid off, then you can switch back to the standard card and save the annual fee.

5. Cash Out Your Savings Accounts: Often people keep money in savings accounts or money markets earning a small amount of interest. If the interest rate on your debt is higher than the rate you're earning on your savings then you are much better off using your savings to pay off that debt faster.

Getting Your Debt Snowball Rolling
by Sarah Milton

Have you ever noticed that hiding from something scary can actually make it scarier? Hiding under the blankets to avoid the monster under the bed doesn't actually make the monster disappear. In fact, it's often not being able to see the monster and the uncertainty attached to where it is, how big it is and what it's doing that sends our brain into a tailspin and makes hiding from it an even scarier experience.

As kids we learn that the best way to vanquish the fear is simply to take a deep breath, come out from under the blanket, flip on the light and check under the bed. Simply put, when you face your fears you tend to find that they're not as scary as your brain suggested they might be.

Whether it's a monster under the bed or a big mountain of consumer debt, the strategy for conquering it is the same; take a good look at what you're dealing with and then attack it with everything you have!

Know Your Monster

The first step is to take an honest look at all your debts. Pull out your credit card bills and other financial statements and write down how much you currently owe to each institution, the interest rate and the minimum monthly payment. Take a look at what you wrote down, ignore the sinking feeling in your stomach and pat yourself on the back for getting out from under the blanket. You just took the first (and biggest) step towards conquering the monster.

Formulate Your Plan of Attack

Take the list of debts and organize them in order from smallest to largest. The interest rates don't matter, only the balances. (It may seem counter-intuitive to attack a balance of $2,000 @ 5% before attacking a $10,000 balance that you're paying 29.9% interest on but put that instinct aside for a second – all will become clear).

Next, take a look at your monthly income and your monthly expenses. Determine how much extra cash flow you have each month and decide how much of that you're prepared to commit to your debt elimination plan. If you don't have any extra cash flow then decide how you can reduce your expenses or increase your income to find some. It doesn't matter how much. Even $50/month will make a surprising impact over time.

Finally, decide what percentage of any 'unanticipated money' (tax refunds, gifts, bonuses etc.) you're going to commit to your debt plan. Once you have those numbers you're ready to start your snowball.

Get Your Debt Snowball Rolling

Like most successful strategies the debt snowball concept is deceptively simple. Pay the minimum payments on each debt every month and then put your extra debt-busting dollars (the amount you allocated from your unpurposed money plus your chosen percentage of any unanticipated money that comes in) against the smallest debt. Do this until the smallest debt is cleared and then take the money that you were using for the minimum payment on that debt, roll it into your snowball and put all that money against the next smallest debt.

As you pay off more debt so the amount that you have available in your snowball to attack the remaining balances increases. This ever increasing amount is at the heart of the strategy and is what makes it so powerful; by the time you get to the biggest debt your payments are much bigger and the debt can be reduced much more quickly than if you'd started with that one at the beginning.

Achieving Smashing Success

The debt snowball strategy works well because eliminating your first (smallest) debt in a relatively short amount of time gives you a strong sense of accomplishment and fires you up to keep going. It can be really disheartening to hack away at a huge balance for 12-15 months and to know that you'll still have it hanging over you for another few months. It's this frustration that derails a lot of people on the path to achieving their goal.

The other advantage to starting small is that when you're fired up by success you tend to get pretty creative in seeking out ways to increase your success even more. It's amazing how many ways you can find to reduce expenses and increase the amount of money you have to apply to eliminating your debts especially when you're close to reaching your goal.

There are a number of websites and blogs written by people who are sharing their journey to debt freedom and you can get some great ideas for saving and creating money from them along with the inspiration and motivation that comes from knowing that other people have overcome the same challenge. All we have to do is work up the courage and motivation to get out from under the blanket and attack our monsters!!

Debt Might Be a Good Reason Not To Save

by Jim Yih

A recent study by Royal Bank is showing that Canadians are having tough time saving money. The study reported that, over the past two years:

- 46% of people have stopped or reduced savings
- Only 12% have increased savings
- 38% of people are not saving money
- Only 33% are saving regularly
- 55% of Canadians find it is hard to be disciplined to a savings habit

Although these statistics might be alarming, should we really be surprised? We live in a society that values consumption. For the past 20 years the solution to economic slowdown was to encourage spending. Spending is the opposite of savings. They are like two heavyweight champs battling it out for the belt and unfortunately, spending is winning the battle.

If you think about it, spending is more natural. It's more fun. It's kind of like a drug, in the sense that spending makes us feel rich and that feeling can be addictive. This is ironic when you consider that the only way to get rich is to save more money and not spend it!

Should People Really Be Saving More Money?

The obvious answer to this question appears be yes but having lots of debt might be a good reason not to be saving money. It's likely that there is greater benefit in paying down debt before you start saving.

Recently I met with a single mother named Jackie who is raising two children on her own. She has accumulated about $20,000 of debt on her personal line of credit and is really stressed about it.

When we look at Jackie's assets, she has $50,000 in RRSPs and $10,000 in a TFSA. She considers her TFSA her emergency money.

If you think about it, it makes no sense for Jackie to have money in savings earning 1% or less when she has debt costing her 5% or more. Every day she has this scenario, she is going backwards financially. Right now, paying down her debts might be Jackie's best form of saving and investing.

Paying Down Debt Can Be One of The Best Investments You Make

My suggestion to Jackie was to take the TFSA and put it right against the line of credit. My justification for this was simple. Every day she has money in the TFSA making about 1.5% she is losing money. She is losing money because her line of credit is costing her 5%. Holding both the savings and the debt at the same time guarantees a profit for the bank and a losing strategy for her money.

If you want to get technical about it, the debt is actually costing her more than 5% on a pre-tax basis. In order to pay down a dollar of interest, on the line of credit, Jackie must make more than a dollar at work because she has to pay tax. In other words, she earns $1.47 to net one dollar after tax.

By using the $10,000 towards debt, she will save $41.67 per month in interest. Keeping the TFSA makes her $12.50 per month in interest which is much less than the before tax cost of not reducing the line of credit.

But What Happens In Case of an Emergency?

Jackie understood the math, but still expressed the concern that she would not have any savings or emergency money.

It's important to remember that by using the TFSA to pay down her line of credit, Jackie has less debt and she can use her line of credit as the emergency fund if necessary. (Note: this strategy only works if you have the discipline to not run up the line of credit again!)

The Bottom Line

Jackie's situation is a perfect example where saving money does not make sense because there is a bigger bang for her buck in paying down debts. I think we forgot somewhere along the line that paying off debts can be one of the easiest and smartest investments we can make. Instead, debt has become big business and financial institutions are quick to encourage us to accumulate more debt as opposed to paying off the debt that we have.

How Much Debt Is Too Much?

by Jim Yih

Many lenders will treat the amount of debt you can afford like a math problem but that doesn't necessarily give you an accurate picture of how much debt you can actually handle.

Lenders use two ratios to determine the amount of debt a borrower can manage: Gross Debt Service Ratio (GDSR) and Total Debt Service Ratio (TDSR). The word "service" refers to monthly payments – the amount of money needed to service (pay) certain expenses such as housing and consumer debt.

Gross Debt Service Ratio (GDSR) looks at the proportion of your income that is required to pay your basic housing costs. It includes the total cost of housing payments (principal, interest, taxes, and heating) divided by the family's total gross income. Your GDSR should not exceed 32%. Spending more than 32% of your gross income on housing expenses can make it difficult to cover other expenses. This is often referred to as having a "housing burden".

Total Debt Service Ratio (TDSR) looks at the proportion of your gross income that is required to cover basic housing costs and all other consumer debts. This is the percentage of your gross monthly income that will be used to cover housing expenses as well as other outstanding loans and debts. Lenders will usually allow up to a 40% TDSR, and it is rare to be able to borrow from a good lender, such as a bank, if your TDSR is above 40%.

Debt in Retirement

Gross income is the term used to refer to the amount of your income before deductions such as income taxes, Canada Pension Plan premiums, Employment Insurance premiums, and workplace benefits. For most borrowers, a TDSR of 40% would equal more than half of their take-home pay. Given that, for most people income declines in retirement, this is an important number to be aware of when planning for retirement. Retirees need to remember that this decline in income will affect their TDSR and, consequently, payments that were manageable before retirement might not be manageable after retirement.

Keep in mind that the GDSR and TDSR are guidelines lenders rely on when extending credit. Consumers need to judge for themselves what amount of debt they can manage. Don't let your lender be the judge of what you can afford. Use your budget and your gut!

Look down the road – are there any factors that may impact how much debt you can afford? Are you planning to help out your kids, start your own business, reduce your work schedule or retire from work? Changes in lifestyle can reduce income and strain the budget. For example, if you are planning to retire in the next few years, borrowing should be limited to what you can afford on your retirement income.

When you are working, your ability to borrow hinges on your employment or self-employment income. In retirement, borrowing will be based on guaranteed forms of income. Lenders consider fixed types of income when extending credit, including work pensions, Canada Pension Plan benefits, Old Age Security, and annuity income. Retirement incomes drawn from investments such as RRSPs, RRIFs, or non-registered investments are neither fixed nor guaranteed, so most lenders exclude them from your income calculation. While you do not want to borrow more than you can afford to pay in retirement, it is easier to establish your access to financing, such as a line of credit, before you retire from work.

If you expect to carry your mortgage or other debt into retirement, before leaving work, it's important to critically analyse whether you can manage your expenses on your retirement income. If it will be tight, discuss with your lender ways to bring your debt in line with your anticipated retirement income. Wait too long and qualifying may be much more complicated.

Once you work out your retirement price tag, it may become clear that your current debt is not manageable in retirement. If you determine that your debt level is too much you should learn ways to manage and reduce debt.

Are You Carrying Too Much Debt?

E.E. Cummings said "I'm living so far beyond my income that we may almost be said to be living apart."

Certain debt management behaviours can indicate if your debt burden is too much. Ask yourself:

- Has your debt been increasing?
- Are you only able to make the minimum payments on your debts?
- Have you missed debt payments or had to take advantage of the "miss-a-payment" feature on your loans or mortgage?
- Are you at or near the limit on most of your credit cards?
- Have you used a cash withdrawal from one credit card or line of credit to pay another?
- Have you obtained new credit because your current credit cards or lines of credit are at the limit?
- Have you borrowed additional money since consolidating your debts?
- Have you received a call from a lender looking for missed payments?

- Have you borrowed money from friends or family to make ends meet?
- Are you unable to set aside even a small amount of savings for a rainy day or emergency?
- Do you feel as though you are living from paycheque to paycheque?

If you answered "yes" to more than a couple of questions, it's time to look at solutions and perhaps get some professional advice. Do not underestimate the value of working with a professional, such as a Financial Counsellor, to find solutions to debt problems and save yourself time, stress, and money. Whatever your situation, there is a solution.

How To Reduce Your Debt
by Jim Yih

Recently I sat down with a couple who had made a New Year's resolution to get serious about tackling their debt and wanted some help.

Take Stock of Your Debt

Before the meeting started, I asked Mike and Jacquie to take stock of their debts by completing a questionnaire I call the Debt Manager. Here's a summary of their debt situation:

The Debt Manager

Name of Debt	Mortgage	Line of Credit	Visa	Store Card	Total
Amount of Debt	$175,000	$34,500	$11,564.33	$4,050.00	$225,114.33
Interest Rate	4.50%	4.0%	18.5%	18.0%	
Minimum Payment	$968.00	$115.00	$231.29	$135.00	$1,449.29
Actual Payment	$1,335.00	$250.00	$500.00	$150.00	$2,235
Time until debt is paid off in full	15 years	15 years 6 months	2 years 5 months	2 years 11 months	
Comment	Paid Monthly	Paid Monthly	Paid Monthly	Paid Monthly	

Can They Afford The Payments?

Currently, Mike and Jacquie are paying $2,235 per month towards their debts. Their take home pay is about $5,000 per month which means 44.7% of their take home pay is going to servicing this debt. No wonder they feel some financial stress from their debts!

In their case though, putting that much of their income towards debt may be a good thing. The main reason for their high payments is that they're paying considerably more than the minimum required and are aggressively paying down their debts.

Strategies to Pay Down Debt Faster

What you have here is a look at a real life case to help you understand the process of assessing your debt situation and developing strategies to tackle the debt problem. Let's take a closer look at Mike and Jacquie's situation and walk through some strategies to get their debt paid down even faster.

Spend Less: The root of a debt problem is often overspending. It's important to fix the overspending problem by spending less before tackling the debt. Mike and Jacquie feel that they have their spending under control now and they're confident that their debt won't get out of hand again.

Consolidation of Credit Card Debts: Jacquie wants to consolidate the two credit card amounts into the line of credit because the interest rates are so much lower on the line of credit. If Mike and Jacquie consolidate the debts into their line of credit, they will have a balance of $50,114.33. If they continue to make the same payments of $900 per month ($250+$500+$150), this loan would be paid off in 5 years and 3 months and their total interest over that period would be $5,413.16. This is a significant savings in total interest from their current strategy which will cost them over $15,800 in interest on the three loans.

Using Savings to Pay Off Debts: Mike has an ING saving account with $4,000 in it making about 1.5%. I suggested that it was mathematically to their advantage to use that $4,000 towards the credit card debt costing 18% instead of keeping it in savings earning 1.5%. Since their debt payments are much greater than the minimum required payments, they have lots of cash flow cushion in case of emergencies. Paying off the store card would immediately save them $1,180 of interest over the next three years and they could also apply the $150 per month towards the Visa card to pay it off six months quicker.

Earn More Income. Jacquie is not working full time. She has stayed at home to raise their two children and has been working part time for the past 18 months. Now that both kids are in school full time, she feels she could work a little more to pay off the debts a little faster. If Jacquie can put an extra $250 per month towards debt payments (assuming the consolidation strategy above) that would knock out the debt 15 months sooner.

Debt Calculators and Tools

To help Mike and Jacquie with the calculations, I used three tools:

The Debt Manager Spreadsheet – This is a simple spreadsheet I put together to help them take stock of their debt and calculate some simple ratios. Feel free to download the spreadsheet from **www.retirehappy.ca/TCOYM.**

Online Debt Payment Calculator– find out how long it will take to pay off debt and how much interest you will pay to do so. (http://www.debtmanagers.ca/debt-calculator.php)

What Will It Take To Pay Off My Debt? – If you have a goal to pay off your credit cards before a specific period of time, you can find out the monthly payment required to pay it off. (http://money.cnn.com/calculator/pf/debt-free/)

Build TFSA or Pay Down Debts?

by Jim Yih

The Tax Free Savings Account (TFSA) is big news in the personal finance world. This tax free account was first introduced in 2009 and it has generated lots of discussions; not only about the TFSA basics but also some new and interesting debates.

Not too long ago, I discussed the new debate as to whether TFSAs or RRSPs are better and I came to the conclusion that both have merits. Just these past couple of weeks, I have run into three situations where people are debating between saving in their TFSAs and paying down debt. Although I'm a big fan of the TFSA, I came to the conclusion that it may make more sense to pay off debts than keep money in the TFSA.

Credit Card Debt vs. TFSA in Savings

Joanne is in her early 30s and she works for a software company. Although she has a $6,500 credit card balance because of a vacation she took this year, she makes enough income to manage the payments and plans to have the balance paid off before the end of the year. Joanne also has $5,000 in her TFSA making less than 1%.

The math is really clear that every day she is paying 18% on her credit cards and making less than 1% in her TFSA, she is making the bank a lot of money. When I suggested that she should cash out the TFSA and put it directly against the credit card balance, Joanne was worried that she would not have any emergency money left. As much as I can appreciate the importance of having an emergency fund, the math suggests that she will have the credit card paid off within two months and then she can aggressively build up her TFSA again.

171

Mortgage vs. TFSA savings

Amanda and Gary are in their early 40s with two children and take an active interest in their financial affairs. They currently have a mortgage of $200,000 at a 4% interest rate and plan to have it paid off in 15 years. Gary contributes about 14% of his pay to RRSPs through payroll deduction and employer contributions. They each have $11,000 in their TFSAs and hope to put another $5,000 lump sum each into the TFSA. Just like Joanne (above), they like the idea of having the TFSA as an emergency fund and as a result, the interest they are making is about 1%.

Although the numbers are not as extreme when comparing the TFSA return to credit card debt, the math still works in favour of paying down the mortgage. If you have an account earning you 1% while having debt that costs you 4%, you are going backwards. Putting the TFSA money towards the debt is the equivalent of earning 4% on the money instead of 1%.

Amanda and Gary have a $25,000 unsecured line of credit in Amanda's name from early in their marriage. They have used this line of credit only once and had it paid off within a few months. Given their discipline and aversion to debt, they are prime candidates to use the line of credit as their emergency fund. For those that lack discipline, using a line of credit can be problematic because the temptation to use the credit for non-emergencies is often too great to resist and debt levels continue to increase.

What Should You Do With Extra Cash Flow?

Melinda and Santos are about 5 years away from retirement. Although they are mortgage free, they do have a $50,000 line of credit that they want to have paid off by the time they retire so they are paying $1,000 per month directly to the line of credit.

They are also putting $500 per month to the TFSA into low interest savings to supplement their retirement spending. Would that $500 per month be used more effectively if it went directly to the line of credit instead of the TFSA?

By putting the $500 per month towards the line of credit, they are earning the equivalent of 5% due to the interest savings. They are not earning anywhere near that in their TFSA. By putting the entire $1,500 per month directly to the debt, they would have it paid off in three years and then they could aggressively build up the TFSA. I've referred to this in the past as the principles of cash flow.

Some Final Thoughts . . .

I run into so many people who are not investing inside their TFSAs. If you are going to keep TFSA money in low interest savings, you may be better off using the money towards paying down debt rather than building up your TFSA.

If you have credit card debt at high interest costs, then no matter what you invest in, you should consider the merits of paying down credit card debt instead of investing in TFSAs.

Although these three examples are based on real life people and real life situations, they merely serve as examples. The best way to tackle any financial debate like the TFSA vs. RRSP or the TFSA vs. paying down debt is to remember that everyone has unique circumstances and individual planning is always recommended

5 Strategies to Manage Your Debt Levels

by Tricia French

Managing debt can be tricky. When thinking about debt in retirement, the best plan is to be debt-free. What would it take for you to dramatically reduce your debt? Could you commit to taking advantage of the extra income you have today and using it to extinguish your debts?

Eliminating Debt

There are many solutions for eliminating your debt. The solution best for you depends on:

- **Amount of Debt** – Larger amounts of debt often require more aggressive solutions.
- **Number of Debts** – Solutions that reduce the number of debts by consolidation may be beneficial.
- **Strength of Credit** – With more established credit, solutions available through a lender, such as consolidation, may be options.
- **Amount of Money Available to Pay Debt** – Finding money in the budget can make paying off loans faster and easier.

Five Key Strategies

1. Increase Income and/or Decrease Expenses: This is an appropriate solution when the debt level is lower or when more money can be made available to pay debts. For example, you could rent a spare bedroom to a student and use the extra income could accelerate the pay down of the household debt. Alternatively, you could simply track your spending and find expenses you can reduce to free up more money to add to your repayment.

2. Refinancing refers to lengthening the duration of a loan in order to reduce the monthly payment. Good credit is essential for this to work, but extending the loan can help the payment "fit" better in your budget.

3. Consolidation is often the preferred solution for reducing the total number of payments and reducing the overall interest. Good credit is vital and collateral (assets) or a co-signer is often required. This solution is especially effective if you have a number of loans or several credit cards with higher interest rates. One loan could pay them off entirely, simplifying several monthly payments into one loan payment at a better interest rate.

Consolidation can be done with a loan or personal line of credit. For home owners, consolidation could happen by way of a home equity line of credit, a second mortgage, or by rewriting the primary mortgage. Rewriting your primary mortgage can result in paying the consolidated debts over the lifetime of your mortgage, costing you a great deal of interest, so proceed cautiously. This solution should be reserved for situations where your budget is so tight, you cannot afford to make all of your payments.

4. Negotiating with Creditors is helpful if you are experiencing a temporary financial setback. You can arrange with creditors to make reduced payments for a short period of time. This option may affect your credit, so attempt the previous options first.

5. Formal and Legislated Insolvency Programs are solutions of last resort. They include Debt Repayment Programs, the Orderly Payment of Debts Program, Consumer Proposal, and Bankruptcy.

Debt can reach an unmanageable level and result in stress that is hard on families. This can happen from taking on too many loans or from a change in circumstances, such as a job-loss or retirement. If your credit has been affected by an inconsistent payment history, you might be unable to take advantage of bank solutions. Legislated programs are available to assist consumers to recover from extreme financial problems and get back on track. Contact Money Mentors (www.moneymentors.ca) or Credit Counselling Canada (www.creditcounsellingcanada.ca) for a list of agencies that offer unbiased information about both formal and legislated programs.

5 Reasons to Pay Off Your Debt ASAP
by Miranda Marquit

In some cases, it's easy to become complacent about debt. After all, many times the individual payments are relatively low and often affordable. Many people don't start feeling real stress about debt until it starts becoming unwieldy but even then, it can be difficult to really buckle down and pay off the debt as fast as possible.

If you really understand how paying off your debt quickly can impact you, though, you will be more inclined to tackle your debt ASAP. Here are five reasons to pay off your debt as quickly as possible:

1. More of Your Money Stays Yours

The reality is that when you pay debt you are paying money to someone else – with nothing in return beyond the privilege of borrowing money. Instead of putting your money toward enriching someone else, you could be using that money to improve your financial situation.

Once your debt is paid off, and you aren't paying that money in interest, you can keep more of your money. If you are feeling overwhelmed with your debt, you can get started right now with help from a service like Consolidated Credit, which can help you see how to keep more of your own money.

2. You Can Start Investing the Money

It's not just about having more of your own money. It's also about using the money to build wealth on your own. Think about how much wealth you could build if you were earning interest from investments, rather than paying interest on debt! The faster you pay off your debt, the more time you have to put the principles of compound interest to work on your behalf.

3. Get Ready for Retirement

One of the reasons that many people aren't prepared for retirement is that they have too much debt to pay off. If you have financial obligations, you will have to work longer and retire later. If you pay off your debt sooner and focus on building your nest egg you can retire when you want – and maybe even retire early.

4. Improved Financial Security

Without obligations hanging over you, the level of your financial security improves. Even if you think that you are doing fine, and that you can handle your current debt payments, think about what might happen if an unexpected setback occurs. Whenever you have debt that is a concern, since your resources aren't going towards shoring up your financial situation.

If you pay off your debt ASAP it allows you to start building an emergency fund to help you weather storms, and you can put more towards creating a secure financial future.

5. Reduce Stress and Improve Your Relationships

Even though you may not realize it, debt puts strain on your relationships. Worrying about obligations – even when they seem "affordable" – can strain your emotions, and your relationships.

Once you pay off debt, a lot of that stress and anxiety disappears. You are able to connect better with your loved ones, and you can handle difficulties better. Paying off debt as quickly as possible brings you relief, and can even improve your relationships.

Don't wait to pay off your debt. Make the arrangements now to do what you can to pay off your debt as quickly as possible. Your finances, and your life, will improve.

Good Debt and Bad Debt

by Jim Yih

When it comes time to spending money, I can still hear my dad saying "Don't spend money you don't have." Unfortunately, spending money we don't have has become all too common. Personal debt is rising too fast and getting credit has become easier than ever.

Few people will argue against the fact that having too much debt is a bad thing; it can be financially destructive. Just look south of the border to see what too much personal debt can do to personal lives, governments and even corporations.

Although too much debt is bad and less debt is good, it is important to understand that there are different types of debt (most of it is bad but some of it is actually good).

Bad Debt

Bad debt is pretty easy to define. It is debt that does not benefit your financial future. Most debt these days is bad debt because it is used to enhance lifestyle as oppose to enhancing wealth. Debt used to buy big screen televisions, furniture, cars and vacations are common examples of lifestyle debt. At the end of your purchase, there is little to no productive wealth to show for your debt. Here are some examples of bad debt:

- **High Interest Debt**: It's pretty obvious that high interest debt is not good. Paying 18% or more is not a good financial strategy. Many credit cards charge ridiculous interest rates and worse yet, too many people keep balances on these high interest cards.

- **Car Debt**: Cars depreciate in value. In other words, you are losing wealth, not gaining it. Canadians love their cars but try living with less car, less debt and drive it longer. Cars are terrible investments. Going into debt to buy a terrible investment is a terrible financial strategy. Living with less car, less debt and driving your car beyond the end of the financing term will help you direct more money to appreciating assets and less to your car.

The best way to avoid bad debt is to start thinking more like my father and others of his generation. It's not fun but there's something smart about it.

Good Debt

Good debt, on the other hand, is debt that is used in financially productive ways. Good debt is debt that creates opportunity to enhance wealth, income or cash flow. Here are some examples:

- **Mortgage**: A mortgage is generally used to buy a home (often your personal home). The reason this is good debt is because you are borrowing money to buy something that appreciates in value. A house is an asset that has value and hopefully increases over time. Home ownership not only is financially productive because real estate increases in value but also because it teaches people to be more fiscally responsible.

- **Leverage**: Leverage is a concept that has been popularized by the financial industry. Financial advisors often promote the merits of borrowing money to invest in stocks or mutual funds. Conceptually, leverage works as long as the investment (after tax) increases in value more than the after tax cost of the interest. The bonus is that, if set up properly, the interest on the loan is tax deductible. Business loans are another example of leverage since the intent is to invest in something that makes money or creates cash flow.

- **Education**: Since your income from work is probably one of the biggest potential contributors to wealth, investing in an education that will give you greater opportunities to earn more income is a good thing. Borrowing to enhance your education can be a form of good debt.

As much as these examples may be good forms of debt, moderation is still the key to financial success. Even good debt can be destructive if you have too much. Just ask people who have bought too much house (or too many houses), borrowed to invest in a terrible investment or who are still paying for student loans long after graduation. At the end of the day, no matter how great the potential benefits, any time you're considering taking on any kind of debt, you need to be sure that carrying it makes sense for your personal situation.

Time to Pay Down Your Mortgages
by Jim Yih

With the recent boom in real estate prices you can pretty much guarantee that most people are carrying more mortgage debt than ever.

In 2001, Canadians collectively held $447.2 billion dollars of mortgage debt. That was a 156% increase over 1982 data when Canadians held $147 billion of mortgage debt. The scary fact is that while mortgage debt increased 156% from 1982 to 2001, disposable income only increased 42%. That means more debt to income than ever before. This trend has to change so in this chapter we're revisiting the issue of whether you're better off to go with a variable rate mortgage or a fixed rate mortgage.

Variable vs. Fixed Rate Mortgages

The debate between variable versus fixed rate mortgages has gone on for a long time. In theory, when interest rates fall many experts will argue that variable rate mortgages will save you interest. However, in rising interest rate environments, fear of never ending increases causes people to lock into 5 year fixed rate mortgages. Recently, Moshe Milevsky, a Professor of Finance at York University presented some research that showed that the variable rate mortgage is, mathematically, the better strategy over 88% of the time.

In Milevsky's research paper, he used interest rate data from 1950 to 2000 to show that Canadians could save $22,000 of interest payments for every $100,000 of mortgage debt over a 15-year amortization by going with the variable rate option.

Pay Fixed Dollar Payments on a Variable Rate

While many people avoid variable rate mortgages because they don't like the idea of variable or changing payments, the secret to using a variable rate is to make payments as if it were a fixed rate payment. Currently the average rate for five year fixed rate mortgages is just under 3.3%. At the same time, the average rate for variable rate mortgages is about 0.6% lower at 2.7%. This current spread of 0.6% between five year fixed mortgages and variable mortgages is not uncommon.

For every $100,000 of borrowed money under a five year fixed rate at 3.3%, the monthly payments would be $488.77. Over a 25-year amortization, you would pay a total of $146,631 in payments of which $46.631 would be interest. With a variable rate of 2.7%, you could have lower monthly payments of $457.99 on the same $100,000. However, instead of going with lower payments, you would be better off to take the variable rate at 2.7% but make monthly payments of the same $488.77 you'd have under the fixed rate option. By paying the $488.77 per month at the lower 2.7% interest rate, you would pay off the mortgage two years sooner. More importantly, you would save $8,000 in interest over the amortization of the mortgage. This approach allows you to blend the security of a fixed rate with the benefit of the lower interest.

Home Equity Lines of Credit (HLOC)

One of the fastest growing trends in the mortgage arena is the explosion of home equity lines of credit. In my mind, HLOCs are a more flexible form of the variable rate mortgage. Interest rates typically float but your payments are extremely flexible. Although HLOCs give you the ultimate in flexibility, that same flexibility can be very dangerous for two reasons. The first is that with HLOCs, it is so easy to go in the wrong direction and accumulate more debt as opposed to paying it off faster. Secondly, it is far too easy for people to only make minimum interest payments and avoid paying down the capital.

With mortgage debt growing faster than ever, it's time for Canadians to get disciplined and start paying down their debts.

It's time for more discipline and less flexibility. You don't have to look very far south to see what too much debt can do to real estate, the economy and people's personal finances.

UNDERSTAND HOW TAX WORKS

"All truths are easy to understand once you discover them; the point is to discover them."

GALILEO

Marginal Tax vs. Average Tax

by Jim Yih

In Canada, we operate under a marginal tax rate system which means that the more money we make, the more tax we are privileged to pay. Marginal tax is simply the amount of tax paid on an additional dollar of income. As income rises, so does the tax rate. This is different than a flat tax rate where you pay the same rate of tax no matter what your income level is.

Knowing your marginal tax rate can help you make effective financial decisions. From a planning point of view it is not good enough to just know how much money you make. It is essential to understand how much you keep. Making a dollar doesn't allow you to count on spending that dollar. Knowing your marginal tax rate will tell you how much of that dollar you can utilize toward your lifestyle. If you are planning your finances or retirement, the focus should be on your net income.

In Canada we have two layers of income tax – federal and provincial. To illustrate how marginal tax rates work, my example shows tax rates for Alberta residents and encompasses both provincial and federal tax.

For the year 2014, there are five tax brackets:

$0 to $11,138	0% (this is not really a bracket but the personal exemption level)
$11,139 to $17,787:	15%
$17,788 to $43,953:	25%
$43,954 to $87,907:	32%
$87,908 to $136,270:	36%
Over $136,270:	39%

So, if live in Alberta and you earned $50,000 in income in 2014, then you would be in the 32% marginal tax If you earned $100,000, then you would be in the 36% marginal tax bracket.

One of the biggest misconceptions about tax rates is that your entire income will be taxed at your marginal tax rate. Here's an example to show you how it actually works:

The person making $50,000 per year would not pay $16,000 in tax ($50,000 x 32%). Instead, his/her tax would be calculated like this:

$11,138 at 0% = $0

$6,649 ($17,787 minus $11,138) at 15% = $997

$24,167 ($43,954 minus $17,787) at 25% = $6,542

$6,046 ($50,000 minus $43,954) at 32% = $1,935

Total tax = $9,474

The marginal tax rate of 32% is the amount of tax paid on each dollar earned between $43,953 and $87,907 (the start of the next tax bracket).

In this example, the average tax is only 18.9% ($9,474 divided by $50,000 of total income). Average tax is the percentage of tax paid based on your total gross income and reflects the total tax you are paying. It is the total amount of tax you will pay through all the brackets divided by total income and will mathematically always be lower than the marginal tax rate.

You can find a comparison chart of Marginal Tax vs. Average Tax online at **www.retirehappy.ca/TCOYM**

The tax system varies from province to province. With 10 provinces and three territories, you can imagine the complexity of the Canadian tax system. Add in the fact that the rules can change every year because of provincial and federal budgets and you have an ever-changing and complex tax system.

Lastly, paying tax is not such a bad thing because it means you are making more money. You hear people complain about paying tax and the desire to pay not tax. I have a solution . . . make only $11,138 a year and you will pay no tax!

Know that no matter what tax bracket you are in, you should never, ever turn down money. Our tax system works in such a way that, even though as you make more money you pay more tax, you will still always be able to put more money in your pocket than if you had turned down a pay raise or overtime. There's no such thing in Canada as a 100% tax bracket. You will never lose by making more money.

My Advice: Learn how the tax system works before you complain and learn how to use the system to your advantage. Rather than trying to spend time trying to predict the future of the markets, invest more time in tax planning because that's time better spent!

A List of Things Not Taxed in Canada
by Jim Yih

In Canada, we pay a lot of tax. In fact, it's been said there are two certainties in life – death and taxes.

Most of your income is taxed at your personal marginal tax rate. Although it's true that we do pay a lot of tax, one of the biggest misconceptions about tax is that half our income goes to taxes.

We hear lots about how much tax we pay (especially at tax time) but I ran across this list of things from Canada Revenue Agency (CRA) that are not taxed. It's not a big list but still a good list to know. When you are doing your tax planning for the future, it's important to be aware of things that are not taxed just as much as it's important to know what is taxed and how it's taxed.

According to CRA, you do not have to include certain amounts in your income, including the following:

- Any GST/HST credit or Canada Child Tax Benefit payments, as well as those from related provincial and territorial programs
- Child assistance payments and the supplement for handicapped children paid by the province of Quebec
- Most amounts received from a Tax Free Savings Account (TFSA)
- Compensation received from a province or territory if you were a victim of a criminal act or a motor vehicle accident
- Lottery winnings
- Most gifts and inheritances
- Amounts paid by Canada or an ally (if the amount is not taxable in that country) for disability or death due to war service

- Most amounts received from a life insurance policy following someone's death
- Most payments of the type commonly referred to as "strike pay" you received from your union, even if you perform picketing duties as a requirement of membership

As I mentioned, this list was taken right from the CRA website. I have one more to add to the list and that is the proceeds from the sale of your principal residence. When you sell property that is not your principal residence, you have to pay capital gains taxes if you sell the property for more than you originally paid for it. (This would include rental property, investment property, and recreational property.) Your principal residence qualifies for a principal residence exemption.

It is important to note that if you invest income sources from any of the above amounts, you will be taxed on earnings. For example, if you won $1 million dollars in a lottery and you invested all or part of the winnings, any investment earnings are taxable.

Not All Income Is Taxed the Same

The best income to have is income that is not taxed. The next best income to have is income that is taxed at a lower rate. I call this tax efficiency. Most income (salary, bonuses, rental income and interest for example) is taxed at your marginal tax rate. Some investment income such as dividends and capital gains is considered "tax preferred" because it is taxed at lower rates which creates greater tax efficiency.

To see the tax benefits of dividend and capital gains income, you can download the Marginal Tax Rate Card at
www.retirehappy.ca/TCOYM

It's Time To Do Some Tax Planning
by Jim Yih

There's no shortage of tax information out there but if you have completed your taxes this year, then tax season has come and gone. Every year tax filers across the country go through the annual ritual of assembling tax receipts to figure out how much we earned and how much tax we will have to pay as a result.

Tax preparation, is really the act of summarizing the historical events of the past year. Typically, tax season is a time to review the past but it is a difficult time to do any strategic planning because it's too late to do things differently. Real tax planning is about looking into the future and trying to develop both long-term and short-term strategies to minimize the tax bill. Now is the time to look ahead in order to develop good planning strategies and habits for the future.

Tax Planning vs. Tax Preparation

There's a big difference between tax preparation and tax planning. Imagine this scenario: You come to a fork in the road. One path has a sign that says "Tax Preparation" and the other has a sign that says "Tax Planning". Which path do you think would get you to financial freedom faster?

If you chose the "Tax Planning" path you're right. This is because planning gives you the ability to implement strategies in the future that will reduce the amount of tax you pay and increase your net income. Unfortunately, this is the path least traveled. Instead, most people journey through life on the path of tax preparation; filing their returns each and every year and getting to their destination whenever they get there. The problem with this approach is that tax preparation is simply the act of filing a return and the strategies needed to reduce your taxes are those that need to be done far in advance. I can't tell you the number of times, I have sat down with people who had no clue about all the tax strategies available to them. Tax preparation is something we all do because we have to. Tax planning, however, is something we should do to help us get to our destination of financial freedom faster.

Getting Planning Advice

Many Canadians, in recognition of their limited understanding of the tax system, will utilize the services of professionals. I am a strong advocate of getting help and advice. Never assume, however, that tax planning will be given without asking.

For example, don't assume your tax preparer will automatically provide tax advice. Sometimes tax preparers aren't qualified to give planning advice. Even Chartered Accountants, who really understand tax planning, may not have time during the tax season to do effective planning with their clients because they may be so busy preparing returns and meeting the filing deadlines. Also, don't assume that the fee paid for tax preparation includes tax planning. Remember, the fee was probably for the time used to prepare the return.

If you have someone who prepares your taxes for you, I would ask them if they do any tax planning and whether you can set up a separate meeting to plan for the future. You might have to pay for their time but chances are it will be worth paying for.

Your financial advisor may or may not provide tax planning advice. Unfortunately, many financial advisors focus primarily on the investment portfolio and products because of the compensation arrangements in the financial services industry. That being said, there are also financial advisors in your community who will help with planning, but you have to ask for assistance in that area.

If the relationship with your advisor has been primarily focused on investment, it may be worthwhile to ask if your advisor does tax or financial planning. If this is not his/her area of interest or expertise, then request a referral to a qualified professional.

Know Your Tax Rates
One of the basic fundamental things you need to know about taxes is your marginal tax rate. For the past four years, I've compiled a one page summary of all of the tax brackets for all provinces and territories in Canada which you can find online at **www.retirehappy.ca/TCOYM**

Other Resources:

www.TaxResource.ca is a great resource with lots of tax planning strategies for Canadians

www.TaxTips.ca has some great tax calculators

Tim Cestnick is one of the most respected tax experts in Canada (http://www.waterstreet.ca/articles.php)

Jamie Golombek is an avid writer and has written extensively on tax planning in Canada (http://www.jamiegolombek.com/index.php)

Three Ds of Tax Planning
by Jim Yih

Tax planning must include strategies to **deduct, defer and divide**. The concept of effective tax planning will have a different meaning and emphasis depending upon your personal circumstances. Add in the fact that governments introduce new tax legislation every year and we begin to understand why Albert Einstein said, "The hardest thing to understand is income tax."

Deduct, Defer and Divide

The three 'Ds' to investing are Deduct, Defer and Divide. You must be able to understand all of these important functions in order to do effective tax planning.

Deduct

A deduction is a claim to reduce your taxable income. A deduction will reduce your tax bill by an amount equal to your marginal tax rate. Some common deductions include:

- Pension plan contributions
- RRSP contributions
- Safety Deposit Box Fees
- Interest expense
- Union/professional dues
- Alimony/maintenance payments
- Employment expenses
- Moving expenses
- Professional fees
- Child care expenses

Defer

A deferral strategy is one that pushes having to pay tax now into future years. Deferring tax means you might eliminate the tax this year but you will eventually have to pay the tax down the road. Generally tax deferral has two advantages:

1. It is better to pay a dollar of tax tomorrow than it is to pay a dollar of tax today.

2. Tax deferral typically puts the control of when you have to pay the tax in the hands of the tax payer instead of in the hands of the Canada Custom Revenue Agency (CCRA).

RRSPs, RESPs and various investment income strategies are the most common forms of tax deferral for the 'average' Canadian.

Divide

Often called income splitting, dividing taxes implies the ability to take an income and spread it among a number of different taxpayers. For example, it you have one person paying tax on $70,000 vs. having two people (say husband and wife) paying tax on $35,000 each, you would rather have the second scenario because the total amount of tax paid on the money would be less.

Unfortunately, you cannot arbitrarily decide who is going to claim what amounts for income, however there are strategies to divide income within the rules of the CCRA:

1. Spousal RRSPs help couples split income in retirement
2. Splitting CPP retirement benefits with your spouse
3. Pension splitting for retired couples
4. Investing non-RRSP savings in name of the lower income family members
5. Investing the child tax benefit in your child's name
6. Utilizing RESP contributions
7. Payment of wages to family members (through a business)
8. Use of partnerships or corporations to earn business

income
9. Utilizing either inter-vivo or testamentary trusts

Jim's Five Cents

I've always said that good tax planning far exceeds good investment planning. While taxation gets more and more complicated with every budget, the fact remains that you must understand the basic concepts of tax deductions, tax deferral and income splitting (dividing).

Sometimes tax planning will bring immediate benefits but often the benefits of tax planning take time to feel the rewards. Many people are scrambling to get their taxes done for the previous year when it is probably too late to do any really effective tax planning.

The Key Foundation Stones to Effective Planning Include:

1. Maintaining and retaining good records
2. Keeping informed and up to date
3. Knowing your needs and your goals
4. Assembling a team of good professional advisors

There's no doubt that tax rules are complicated; in the words of Marc Denhez "Anyone who believes that Canada's only two official languages are English and French has never read the Income Tax Act." If you are confused by the tax act and all the different rules then it makes sense to seek the help of a qualified professional to help you do some effective tax planning.

GETTING HELP FROM OTHERS

"At the end of the day, the questions we ask of ourselves determine the type of people that we will become."

LEO BABAUTA

Who's Your Money Mentor?

by Sarah Milton

The way that we handle money as adults is greatly influenced by everything we hear, see and experience in relation to money while we are growing up. For many people the money messages that they receive as children are a confusing and mostly negative combination and this often leads to challenges in managing money effectively as adults.

As human beings we're hard-wired for pleasure; we like to spend time on things that we enjoy and we can get very creative when it comes to avoiding things that we find difficult or complicated. This is a problem when it comes to finances because if you're not paying attention to your money there's a good chance it's not working as hard for you as it could be. Even when you have good role models, the challenge comes in moving past the limits of their expertise and continuing on the path to building wealth.

I've been thinking a lot this week about finding role models and mentors in the areas of my life where I'm looking to make the most change. I'm starting to see very clearly how the people we surround ourselves with can be instrumental in determining whether or not we succeed and to understand just how critical it is to surround ourselves with people who will help us soar rather than help us make excuses to stay grounded. This is especially important when it comes finding a money mentor because our financial health has a huge impact on our overall wellbeing and our ability to live the life we dream of.

A mentor is defined as a "wise and trusted counsellor or teacher, someone willing to spend their time and expertise to guide the development of another person" and they come in all shapes and sizes.

Family

Our families tend to be the first money mentors. Watching the way that the adults who raise us handle their money helps us form our first opinions about money, wealth and rich people. Our financial goals as young adults often mirror the goals and values of the adults who influenced us most as children. This can be either positive or negative, depending on how financially savvy those adults were.

As parents, it's important not only to teach our children how to manage their money well but also to model that behaviour for them as well. Our actions really do speak much louder than our words; children learn far more from what they see than they do from what we say.

Friends

Our friends are a great source of information and advice, even when we don't ask for it. Unfortunately, our friends are also adept at helping us justify unnecessary expenses or indulgences and they're often the reason that we're tempted into a spontaneous night out or an extra trip to the liquor store! It's said that we're the sum of the five people we spend the most time with and this is especially true when it comes to finances.

If we spend time with people who value money and are committed to building wealth then there's a good chance that we will manage our money in a similar way. If most of our close friends love to spend more than they love to save then there's a good chance that we will do the same. Choosing to spend time with people whose outlook on life is similar to ours makes it easier to reach our goals and reduces the chances that we'll sabotage ourselves once we start to move into a space which is much different from where we started.

A money mentor can help affirm our positive choices and inspire us to avoid making the choices that take us further away from our goals.

Choosing The Right Money Mentor

When it comes to choosing a money mentor, look for someone who already has what you are working towards. Choosing someone with similar values and a similar approach to life means that there's a good chance that they will understand your motivators because theirs will be similar. If you can't find anyone amongst your family and friends who would make a good mentor then you may need to move outside of your social circle in order to find them.

It's said that "when the student is ready, the teacher will appear" and I'm discovering in my own life right now how true that is. As children we're encouraged to ask adults for advice and information and yet for some reason once we become adults ourselves we often feel as though we're supposed to magically know everything about everything, especially when it comes to money, and so we stop asking. It seems though, that the people who learn the most, ask the most questions so finding someone with the experience and expertise to answer those questions seems like a smart move. What do you think?

The Value of a Financial Mentor
by Sarah Milton

A wise woman told me several years ago that if I wanted to get ahead I should find someone who had already achieved what I was working towards and learn from their journey. It was good advice that has helped me in achieving many of my personal and career goals and it's a tip that I've shared many times with others.

Sometimes the idea of asking for advice or mentorship from someone who is more successful than we are can be intimidating. We're so conscious of the ways in which we're lacking that we feel as if we're imposing on the person we're seeking advice from. The reality though, is that having the opportunity to offer advice and coaching is often just as rewarding to the person doing the mentoring as it is to the person being mentored. There's a good chance that the person giving the advice was once helped in a similar way and having the chance to share knowledge and offer insights to someone else is a great way to pay forward the benefits they received.

When it comes to your finances; learning from people who have knowledge that you don't can be a great way to build wealth and boost your level of financial education.

Choose Your Financial Mentor Carefully

Money is a fact of life; we have to handle it on a daily basis whether we enjoy it or not but people are driven by different reasons to build wealth. When it comes to choosing a financial mentor make sure you choose someone who enjoys money and is building wealth for reasons that motivate you too. If you see building wealth as a great strategy for being able to impact others, find a mentor who is committed to philanthropy. If you love the lifestyle and the "stuff" that having money allows then choose a mentor who is living the lifestyle that you aspire to. Whether you choose a mentor from your local community or choose to follow in the footsteps of an author or speaker you admire, as long as their vision and their personality resonates with you it will be a great learning experience.

Make Your Financial Goals SMART

As with any goal it's important to ensure that the financial goals you set for yourself are **S**pecific, **M**easurable, **A**chievable and **R**ealistic within a given **T**imeframe. Your mentor's experiences will open your eyes to what it's possible to achieve as well as help you identify what your motivator is for achieving that goal. Once you have clearly defined your goals, you can develop a plan to get you from where you are to where you want to go. Your mentor's success will make your own goals seem even more possible and their experiences will help you to anticipate obstacles and to develop strategies to overcome them, further increasing your chances of success.

Expand Your Horizons

One advantage of working with a financial mentor is that they open your eyes to a new reality and make new things seem possible. I heard a speaker say during a seminar that we are the sum of the five people we spend the most time with and I think there's a lot of truth in that.

Often the people we spend the most time with are people from similar backgrounds, with similar education who are in similar financial situations. It's comfortable to be around people we feel equal to but if we aspire to be somewhere else then we need to expand our horizons. Spending time with new people in new places can be uncomfortable at first but it's surprising how quickly we adjust. Pay attention to how your mentor spends their time, the people they associate with, the organizations they're involved with and the sources they use to boost their financial education. By following in their footsteps, you're creating habits that will form a solid foundation for your future success.

Don't be Afraid to Move On

It's said that people come into your life for a reason, a season or a lifetime and when you know which it is, you know what to do. This is just as true for mentorships as it is for any other relationship. Your journey to financial success may involve learning from more than one teacher so being open to the idea that it may be time to find a new mentor makes it easier to move on when the time is right.

Whether your financial mentor is a friend, co-worker, financial advisor or another successful individual, there is much value to be found in aligning yourself with someone who has already achieved what you are working towards.

Why not take some time this week to look over your financial goals and to think about who you know (or who you could get to know) who might be open to giving you advice or providing an example that would help you in your journey. If you have a mentor story you'd like to share, let me know, I'd love to hear it.

Do-It-Yourself or Financial Advisor?

by Jim Yih

This debate is getting more and more heated. There is no shortage of different perspectives on the issue of looking after your own money versus using a financial advisor. Here's my perspective on this debate.

Doing It On Your Own

When I first started in this business 23 years ago, I could read a couple of newspapers and a few industry publications a day and I typically had more information than most investors.

Today, we live in a world of information overload and most of that information is free. With the development of the internet, investors and readers have access to the exact same information that any financial advisor might have. There are lots of publications you can subscribe to that are designed to appeal to the investor who wants to take a "do-it-yourself" approach.

However, this "free world of information" has created its own problems in that there is now too much information – just like there are too many mutual funds. As someone in the financial industry, even I find it incredibly difficult to keep up with all the information. And really, who can keep up?

This has made the world of investing confusing and complex. So what's my point? Investing requires five basic requirements:

1. **Access to Information**: There is an overwhelming amount of financial information online and all the average investor needs is a computer and an internet connection in order to access it. Google investing and you will find incredible amounts of information on taxes, stocks, mutual funds and investing. If you are a regular visitor of about three to five

quality websites, you will have access to more than enough information to do-it-yourself.

2. **Desire to Seek That Information**: Here is the reality . . . some people love investing as much as I love to garden . . . and I hate gardening. If you are a gardener, please do not take offense at that; it's just not my thing. Similarly, while I love personal finance and investing I know many people who have no desire, motivation or passion for this topic. In order to invest on your own, you must want to learn more and keep abreast of new information. The fact is that not all people will share this 'want' and they are likely the people who should seek the help of a financial advisor.

3. **Time to Find That Information**: The problem is no longer having access to information. Rather it is two-fold: Firstly, you must find the time to be able to research and seek the right information. For those of you who are do-it-yourselfers already, you probably devote a reasonable amount of your free time to reading books, magazines or surfing the internet. You may not do it regularly but there are points in time, like RRSP season, where you will devote more time to the subject. Secondly, you must filter the information. This will be a very challenging aspect too. With free access to endless amount of information, there is also a lot of 'bad' information out there. The scam artists are more abundant than ever and you must be able to filter out the good from the bad.

4. **Access to the Information**: While there is a lot of free information out there, there is also software and subscriptions that make researching that much easier. Some financial advisors have access to significant resources including software and publications on financial planning, investment planning and retirement planning.

Sometimes this information is catered to professionals only. If you are going to do-it-yourself, I would suggest investing not only time but also some money into books, software, and subscription services.

5. **Create a Money Network**: I find the most successful investors not only read and research but they have networks of people to bounce ideas off. If you are going to do it on your own, try to find some other "do-it-yourselfers" to discuss ideas and information. There are several 'non-professional' investors who have created wonderful blogs to help the do-it-yourself investor.

Finding the Right Financial Advisor
by Jim Yih

If you're not a "do it yourself" investor, you will have to find the right person to help you out. Unfortunately, this search can be as challenging as trying to find the best investment.

Just like there are good investments and there are bad investments, the same applies to financial advisors. There are good advisors and there are bad advisors. So what makes a good advisor? It is a tough question to answer but the tougher aspect is to try to find that person to work with.

My criticism of the financial industry is that it is still too easy to become a financial advisor. Take a couple of exams and you are now qualified to sell investment products.

In my travels, I speak to many investors about how to make better financial and investment decisions. In the last couple of years, I have spent more time speaking to financial advisors about how to be better financial advisors. I've thought long and hard about this issue and I offer you some of my thoughts:

1. **Good Advisors Possess 'The Five Qualities'**: A good advisor has the time, expertise, knowledge, resources and passion to invest. Those qualities are necessary to become a good investor and they must also exist in a good advisor. I have met many advisors who lack these qualities and they give my industry a bad name.

2. **Good Advice Goes Far Beyond Investing**: Most people go to financial advisors to help them invest money. The reality is good financial planning and good tax planning goes much farther than good investment planning. A good financial advisor will recognize this truth.

   In my opinion, good financial planning can benefit you by

10% to 50% but good investment planning can benefit you by 1% to 5%. It doesn't take a rocket scientist to figure out which has more value!

3. **Product vs. Advice**: A good financial advisor will recognize that advice is their distinguishing characteristic. Products are simply tools; a good advisor knows where those tools fit and when to use them. Far too many advisors focus on the tools because they focus too much on how they are going to get paid.

   The best financial advisors across the country focus more on giving good advice and the products are simply an extension of that advice. If you are concerned about objectivity of advice, recognize that there are more and more financial advisors (even full service) who offer mutual funds on a no load basis. In the future there will also be a greater number of fee-for-service brokers who will charge for advice and not product.

In the end, it boils down to two key issues: trust and competence. You must find a financial advisor who is competent in his or her field. Some objective qualities to look for are education, experience, industry association membership, and references. You must also trust this person. A financial advisor handles one of the most important tangible assets in your life. Ask yourself if you can see yourself working with this person for a long period of time. Unfortunately, finding this financial advisor is not easy.

Whether you invest on your own or you have a good relationship with your advisor, I wish you much satisfaction and prosperity in your investing future.

Tips For Finding A Financial Advisor
by Jim Yih

Most people would agree that finding a good financial advisor is pretty important. Sound financial advice can make big differences in your financial future. It can be the difference between financial freedom and just making ends meet; or the difference between early retirement and working in the golden years; or maybe the difference between peace of mind and financial disaster. Unfortunately, finding a good financial advisor can also be extremely difficult. Here are five simple tips to help you find good professional advice.

1. Be Prepared: Start with knowing what you want and don't want from an advisor. Everyone is at different financial stages of life. Some people need financial advisors to help with life insurance because they have young families. Others need investment advice for their sizeable portfolios. Some want to create retirement income in their golden years. Whatever the case may be, you can't get proper help without being able to articulate what you are looking for.

2. Get a Referral: There are thousands of advisors in your area. Picking an advisor from the Yellow Pages is like finding a needle in a haystack. In most cases, it's a hit and miss strategy. The better way to find an advisor is through word of mouth. If you want a great advisor, ask your friends and family if they are dealing with a great advisor. If you manage to get a good referral, be sure to ask why they think their advisor is great. This question may be more important than the first because it will provide some details and insights as to what makes the advisor special and different.

3. Interview Multiple Advisors: Even if you get a good referral to a great advisor, how do you know if that advisor is right for you?

Finding the right advisor means meeting and talking to more than one advisor. You should never feel obligated to deal with the first advisor you interview. Interviewing multiple advisors allows you to compare their strengths and weaknesses. Interviewing is like research; the more you do, the more likely you are to make better decisions. I suggest interviewing three advisors.

4. Recognize That There Are Generalists and Specialist: The term financial advisor is too generic these days. Many financial advisors will tell you that their services extend from basic financial planning to investment management to retirement planning or estate planning and they can sell you anything from life insurance to mutual funds.

One stop shopping with a generalist has some advantages but recognize there are times when you should be dealing with experts. If you are looking to invest in mutual funds, wouldn't it make sense to talk to a financial advisor who really understands investing as opposed to someone who specializes in insurance and estate planning? Don't be afraid to ask a financial advisor what they are good at. In fact, you should ask if they have a specialization; their strengths will benefit you.

5. Focus On the Person and Not the Company: Far too often, people choose to deal with a company like a bank as opposed to a specific advisor. The law of averages says that every company has good advisors and bad advisors. Over time most advisors will move companies so staying loyal to a company often means dealing with multiple advisors. Sometimes you may get one of the good reps but other times, you may not be so lucky.

It is more important to build a relationship with a person than a company so find someone you can develop a long term relationship with regardless of what company they work for. Finding the right advisor might take work but it's worth it.

Questions To Ask Financial Advisors Before You Hire Them
by Jim Yih

When it comes to investing, some people are capable of being the "do-it-yourselfer" while others need the help of a financial advisor. Finding the right financial advisor to work with has become just as challenging as trying to pick the right investment. There are more advisors than ever and their roles are not always clear.

Interviewing Financial Advisors

I meet a lot of people who go out and interview one financial advisor and then their decision is either yes or no. The best thing you can do is give yourself choice by interviewing more than one financial advisor. Not all financial advisors are created equal so you have to learn to interview them. Here's a bunch of questions to help you determine the right advisor to hire.

Questions About The Advisor

1. How long have you been in business?

2. Do you specialize in anything?

3. What do you like most about being an advisor?

4. What educational designations do you have?

5. What makes you different from all the other advisors that are out there?

Questions About Their Business

6. What does your organization look like?

7. How many clients do you have?

8. What does your ideal client look like?

Questions About Products And Services

9. What are your product biases?

10. What kinds of products do you sell?

11. What kinds of products can you not sell?

12. What services do you provide?

13. What is your area of expertise?

14. Do you do financial/retirement plans?

Questions About Investing

15. What is your investment philosophy?

16. What do you do for investment research?

17. How do you choose investments to buy?

18. When do you sell investments and why? What is your sell strategy?

19. How often do you trade? And why?

20. What is your track record?

21. Do you have an example of a model portfolio?

22. How do you measure or judge performance?

23. Do you use performance benchmarks?

24. How do you measure risk?

25. How do you define risk?

26. What measures do you use to evaluate risk?

27. What is your position on taxation of investments?

28. Will I have an investment plan?

29. What will that plan entail?

30. What is the process I will have to go through?

31. Do you use investment policy statements?

Questions About Compensation And Service

32. How do you get paid?

33. What fees do you charge?

34. What total fees will I have to pay directly or indirectly?

35. How often will you report back to me?

36. What is your preferred method of communication?

37. What is your service proposition?

38. How often will my portfolio be reviewed?

39. Do you have client references?

40. Ask them to explain a concept to you.

41. When is the best time to invest?

42. What is the best way to save money on tax?

43. Can you explain the difference between RRSPs and TFSAs?

Developing an Interview Process

There are a lot of questions here and, depending on the length of the meeting, you may not want to ask all of them. Choose the questions that are most important to you and type them out (leave room for notes). Take this document into the interview and let the advisor know you have some questions, then take notes as the advisor answers them.

As soon as you are done the meeting, take a moment in private to rate how the advisor did with each of the questions. I like to use a scale of 1 to 10. It's important to do this right away while everything is fresh in your head.

Once you have interviewed two or three advisors, you can now use these documents to compare them. Here are the three most important questions of all:

- **Can you see yourself developing a long term relationship with this advisor?**

- **Do you trust this advisor?**

- **Can this advisor fulfil your financial needs over the next five to 10 years?**

Can you think of other questions that are important to ask financial advisors before you hire them? Note them below so you don't forget!

TAKING ACTION

"Nobody can go back and start a new beginning, but anyone can start today and make a new ending."

MARIA ROBINSON

Do You BELIEVE You Can Become Wealthy?

by Jim Yih

Like him or not, T.Harv Eker has become one of the leading experts on the psychology of wealth and money. He believes financial success comes from working on the "inner game" of money and, when combined with the outer game (the tools), results skyrocket.

It All Starts With Belief

For most people, the biggest hurdle to wealth comes from lack of belief that it is possible to achieve wealth. If you don't think you are worthy of wealth, you have a problem.

Don't get me wrong, I am not one of these motivational gurus who thinks if you believe you can be wealthy, it will automatically happen. Building wealth may be simple, but it's not that easy. But I do think that if you believe you can't become wealthy, then you probably won't. It reminds me of Henry Ford's famous quote "Whether you think you can or can't, you are right."

If you start with negative beliefs about money, it is difficult to get more of it. For example, some people think 'money is bad' or 'people with money are crooks' or 'money is the root of all evil'. If you think this way, it may be hard to rationalize having more wealth with these negative hurdles in the way.

I believe a wealth mindset starts with believing that wealth can be good, productive and also attainable. If you don't think this way, how can you want to be wealthier? Here are a few of my thoughts on wealth and money.

Wealth Is Attainable

Sometimes we perceive wealth as something you inherit or something you get if you are really lucky but statistics show that more people achieve wealth by working hard and saving money than people who inherit it or win it in a lottery. Some stats suggest that 80% of the wealthy made it one dollar at a time while less than 10% inherited it or got lucky.

Luck Is Created

If you have not achieved wealth and success, then maybe consider that your current or old ways of doing things have gotten you to where you are now. If you want different results, then you probably need to consider doing different things. Remember the definition of insanity is doing the same things over and over again and expecting different results. For many people luck is created. It's funny how the harder I work, the luckier I get.

Selective Retention

Sometimes people search for the answers in life but when the answers don't 'fit' with their current ways of thinking, then they simply ignore them and continue searching. Maybe the answers have been there all along but you just haven't recognized them.

You Have To Really Believe!

The mind is very powerful. It operates at both the conscious and the sub-conscious level. Some people try to believe it is possible to become rich but it sits at the conscious level. For example, I know many people who read books on wealth, attend seminars, and believe they will become wealthy. Yet they still have money problems. True success comes when your belief moves from the conscious to the sub-conscious level.

Change Can Be Uncomfortable

To a certain extent, we are all creatures of habit. I'm not saying that people are not impulsive or do not like to try new things from time to time but if you really analyse your life, I suspect a lot of your life is built around patterns. Do you take the same route to work the same way every single day? Do you have 250 TV channels and watch the same 10 all the time? Do you have a wardrobe of clothes and yet wear the same 20% most of the time? Do you go to the same restaurants most of the time? And order the same item off the menu most of the time? Do you cook the same meals repeatedly?

As much as change can be uncomfortable, change can also good especially if it means improvement. I've always agreed with Mark Twain's comment that, "if you always DO what you've always DONE, you will always GET what you've always GOT." If you want something different, then change is inevitable.

It's not what we don't know that prevents us from succeeding, sometimes it's the stuff we know but do not put into action that is our greatest hurdle to success. Lack of action can be a big problem. If you think about it, wealth is built on a foundation of strong money habits and those habits are rooted in the belief that implementing them has a real chance of leading to financial success. Belief alone won't get you to your goal but a firm belief combined with committed action can lead to great things.

Get Serious About Your Finances
by Jim Yih

This year, I started with a long overdue physical at the doctors. No surprise, the doctor said to me it's time to get serious about losing some weight. As I reflect back on some of the things my doctor said I needed to do to lose weight, there seemed to be a lot of parallels to the advice I often give to people who want to get serious about getting their financial affairs in order.

1. Know What You Are Worth

The starting point of any financial plan is to understand your net worth. Your net worth is simply what you own less what you owe. Understanding your net worth is no different than me stepping on the scale at the doctor's office. Knowing my weight establishes a measurable benchmark so I can understand how I am doing in the future (gaining weight means I am doing the wrong things). For most people, the goal is to increase your net worth year after year. Although I may stand on the scale to check my weight weekly, checking your net worth probably only needs to happen once a year.

2. Know How Much Money You Spend

Most people I meet don't know how much money they spend on a monthly or yearly basis. The ones that think they know how much they spend sort of know but typically underestimate. Very few people know what they are spending and the ones that do, typically are in pretty good financial shape. Tracking expenses is kind of like tracking your calories. My doctor talked about starting with the basics of knowing how many calories I should be eating in a day. In order to know how many calories I take in a day, I also need to understand and monitor the caloric values of everything I eat. Now this was a learning curve. After learning about caloric values and portion sizes, it's been much easier to monitor my calorie intake in a day. No different than tracking expenses, it takes effort, conscious awareness and ongoing work. Maybe that's why most people don't track expenses or calories?

3. Make Yourself Accountable

Self-discipline is such a tough thing. It's especially tough in a world that promotes indulgence, choice and convenience. We live in a world where it's so easy to spend money you don't have. You may want to save money but it is so much easier (and more fun) to spend now and plan to save later. If you think about it, it's no different than trying to lose weight. Sometimes it's just a lot easier to run through the drive thru and pick up a burger than it is to make a healthy meal at home. My doctor has scheduled a three month follow up to see how my progress is doing. What he is really doing is creating accountability. If you want to get serious about finances, it starts with yourself. You have to create the motivation to change but sometimes it helps to get some help along the way. Get someone to help you be accountable. This might be your spouse or a sibling or a friend.

At the end of the day, my doctor says losing weight is one thing but keeping the weight off long term is about a change in lifestyle. Losing too much weight too fast is dieting and most people who diet gain back the weight they lost and more. Losing a little weight over a long period of time is much better because it is usually the result of a change in permanent change in lifestyle rather than a temporary change in eating habits. Getting serious about finances is no different. Those that get lured into hot tips or get rich quick schemes rarely get there as fast as they want. Most people get rich the slow and steady way; one dollar at a time.

Feel the Fear and Do It Anyway!
by Sarah Milton

In October 2012, I checked goal number 85 off my 101 Lifetime Goals list: I jumped out of a perfectly good airplane at 13,500ft; freefalling for 60 seconds at 120 mph before spending 5 minutes drifting the final 4000 ft. down to earth under canopy as the sun set over Lake Simcoe.

It was an incredible experience, especially as I'm not exactly a daredevil (I'm more than a little nervous of heights and have never even ridden a rollercoaster) and it taught me that not only can fear keep you from experiencing some amazing things but also you don't know what you're capable of until you try.

When it comes to money and finances, too often people are willing to stay in a situation that is less than ideal in order to avoid the potential pain of trying something new. Whether you've reached a point where the discomfort is too much to stand or you're so irritated you just have to make a change it can still be intimidating to take the first step.

Continuing to hold onto a habit or belief that no longer serves you is never a good way of achieving your dreams and with a little research and some careful planning you can minimize the risks and maximize your potential for success. When I reflected on the process of planning my jump I realized that there were two principles that applied as much to planning a financial habit change as they did to skydiving:

Understand Your Motivation

Why do you want to make the leap? What are the benefits to your current situation of making the change? Maybe you're carrying too much debt or maybe you're not committing as much as you could to reaching a savings goal. Making a change might require some discomfort as you re-purpose your income or take on another job in order to meet your goals. Ask yourself if the short term pain will make the long term gain worthwhile? Is your drive to achieve your goal enough that when you feel the discomfort you'll resist the temptation to give up on the change and go back to your original state?

For me, I'd wanted to do the jump for a long time and I'd made a commitment that 2012 would be my year to conquer fears in all aspects of my life. I booked my first public speaking engagement for September and the thought of being on stage in front of a room full of people terrified me so much that I figured the best way to get past it was to commit to something even scarier! It sounds a little loopy but it worked; every time I got nervous about the event I reminded myself that compared to falling 13,500 feet from a plane it really wasn't that bad! The seminar went fabulously and I discovered a passion for skydiving.

Do Your Research

I'm the last person to bash the joy of spontaneity (I'm a red-haired Sagittarius, so impulsiveness is in my nature) but I've learned the hard way that most of the time it's better to have a plan. This is especially true when it comes to finances. Take the time to think about what it is you want to achieve, why you want it and how you're going to get there.

Make sure that your goals are S.M.A.R.T., seek advice from professionals and then do research of your own and go back with any questions you might have.

Preparation and forward planning help ensure that your plan fits your goals and maximize your chances of financial success. When it came to making my jump I chose a reputable company who I'd researched and been recommended by friends. I jumped tandem with an instructor who'd completed more than 2500 jumps and yes, the risks were definitely there (and very clearly laid out in the pages of waivers I signed before suiting up) but the odds were in my favour and the experience was amazing.

Making an informed decision in order to achieve a clearly defined purpose under the guidance of a qualified professional you trust dramatically increases your chances of success. There are never any guarantees but life would be pretty boring if everything always went according to plan and it's surprisingly how often we learn to fly from falling.

At the end of the day managing your money well is key to building financial success but it doesn't need to be complicated and it can even be a lot of fun. Just remember: it's not rocket science, it's pocket science!

Financial Planning Is A Road Map To Financial Freedom

by Jim Yih

Financial planning is a broad, generic term that can mean different things to different people. Too often, it is associated with financial products like mutual funds or life insurance. For others, it's simply about getting ahead financially.

If you Google "financial planning," you will find a lot of attempts at explaining what financial planning is. Despite the fact that there is no shortage of information about what financial planning is or should be, it is still confusing to many people. Even I have had struggles with explaining what financial planning means.

Financial Planning Is A Road Map

The word 'planning' means looking into the future to make the future as predictable as possible. That's all plans are - a road map or game plan or framework for the future. Add the word 'financial' and a financial plan is simply a look into your financial future to ensure that you are implementing the right financial strategies to get ahead financially.

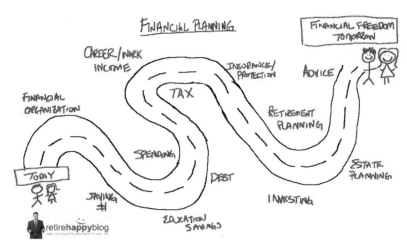

A road is a strong metaphor for a plan. Most roads have a starting point (where you are today) and a destination (where that road will take you). Often roads have intersections where you can get off the road you are on and get onto a different road. A road sets a direction, which is likely to change from time to time. All of these thoughts are also relevant to financial planning.

As you can see in the diagram on the previous page, financial planning is a journey. It's not just a destination but also a series of destinations through a journey . . . a financial journey. Along the way, there are a number of different issues or what I call priorities to take into consideration.

The 12 Priorities of Financial Planning

1. Financial Organization

How organized are you? Are you dealing with the basics of money management like using a net worth statement, cash flow statements, budgeting and paper management?

2. Debt management

Are you in control of your debt? Do you know how to reduce, manage and pay down your debts like mortgage, credit cards, lines of credit, etc.?

3. Managing Your Spending

Do you live within your means? Are you an overspender? Do you need to learn about budgeting and expense tracking? Are you in control over your spending?

4. Saving Money

Do you save money regularly? Do you know how much you should save? Do you know if you are using the right accounts like RRSPs or TFSAs? When will you have enough saved?

5. Career and Work

Are you happy with your work? Are you making enough income? Do you have a plan for how you can progress in your career and boost your income?

6. Risk Management

Are you protected from financial disaster? Do you have enough life insurance? Do you have disability coverage? Do you have an emergency fund? Are you prepared for a rainy day?

7. Investing

Do you know what you are invested in? Do you participate in the management of your portfolio? How is your portfolio doing? Have you reviewed your portfolio lately?

8. Tax Planning

How much tax are you paying? How much do you keep after tax? Do you do tax planning? Are you taking advantage of tax savings strategies?

9. Retirement Planning

Do you have a retirement plan? Do you know when you want to retire? Can you retire? Do you know how much money you will need or have at retirement?

10. Estate Planning

Have you thought about an estate plan? Do you have a will, an enduring power of attorney and a personal directives? Have you thought about what will happen if you die or become disabled?

11. Saving For Children's Education

If you have children, have you thought about who is going to pay for their education? Are you utilizing RESPs? Have you looked at other ways to save?

12. Working With Advisors

Do you need help from a professional? Do you work with a financial advisor? How do you find a good advisor? How do you work with them? How do you pay them?

What Are Your Priorities?

At different stages of life, you will have different financial priorities. The things that matter most when you are in your 20s may not be the same as what matters most when you are 55 or 85.

Financial planning is really about assessing your priorities at different stages of your life and setting some goals and direction based on those priorities. Financial planning is about assessing where you are and where you want to be and then setting some priorities and goals along the way as you journey on the road to financial freedom (whatever that means to you).

If you want help assessing where you are today and setting some goals to start the journey, you can download the Financial Goals and Priorities Worksheet assessment I use with people at **www.retirehappy.ca/TCOYM**

Developing Financial Routines for Financial Success

by Jim Yih

In finances, just as in life, routines are important in order to create the order that leads to success. As a father of four young boys, the summer is a time when we stay up a little later and the kids can sleep in as a result. When school starts up again though, it's important for us to get the kids back on to a regular routine. I think routines are essential not just for the kids but also for the parents. In fact I think most people need some routines in life. Routines are like habits, they are things you do over and over again without really thinking about them. Routines can make life more comfortable.

What Are Your Current Financial Routines?

Take a moment and think about your regular financial routines. Do you have a system for paying the bills? How about going to the bank? Do you actually go to a teller and talk to the same people routinely? How do you check your bank account? Do you have any routines with regards to your investments? Do you check your investment account balance regularly? Do you have a system to review your investments? Are you in a routine when it comes to updating your net worth statement? What about your financial routines around budgeting or spending?

It's important to assess your current financial routines and think about whether they are good routines or bad routines. The routines that come to mind first are likely habits that are subconscious. In other words you just do them because you have trained your mind and body to do these automatically. These routines play a big role in your financial success.

228

Identify New Desired Routines

Once you understand your current routines, the next step is to see if you have any financial issues that you want to address. The best way to address them is to develop a productive routine around solving the problem. I'll give two common examples I see with people.

1. Julie has a spending problem and she is constantly over spending. She needs to come up with a solution that breaks her routine of shopping by developing a new routine that helps her break the old habit. Every person is unique and different so it's difficult to solve a problem with a specific universal solution but here are some ideas for Julie:

- Write down everything she spends and once she reaches a dollar threshold, she has to stop spending. The routine of writing everything down will make her aware of her spending and soon tracking it will become second nature.

- Julie could ditch the habit of killing time by wandering around the mall or through her favourite store and find another routine that doesn't tempt her to overspend.

- Cutting up the credit card is an example of a strategy to break the old routine. We live in a society where it is so easy to spend money we do not have. Cutting up her credit cards may help Julie to resist common problem of overspending. If she can't bring herself to cut up her cards she could try taking them out of her wallet and giving them to someone she trusts to keep them away from her. She could also put them inside a Ziploc bag of water and hide them in the freezer so she has to defrost them before she can use them... this literally creates a 'cooling off' period between seeing an item and buying it!

2. Ned is a decent saver and has accumulated a portfolio that he has neglected for many years. He has realized that he now has about $150,000 saved up through his Group RRSP plan at work and has never really paid any attention to the portfolio. Ned wants to get into a routine of checking his investments more frequently and developing a strategy to improve returns.

Ned's sister Nancy has a routine that she shared with Ned. Nancy was checking her portfolio once a month and inputting the values into a spreadsheet so she could see how her investments changed over time. By doing this with her portfolio, she was able to tell exactly how much money she had and which investments were performing better or worse than others.

Ned thought this was a great idea and committed to the financial routine of scheduling a time in his calendar to log into the company website and look at his investments at the end of every month.

Routines are an important part of your financial success. Having good routines creates more engagement and awareness about your money. The better your financial routines, the better your finances will be. Remember, the more you take care of your money, the more your money can take care of you in the future.

Will Your Routines Change In Retirement?

Retirement is a different phase of your life and as a result sometimes the financial routines you had while you were working may not be the best financial routines to have when you are retired. Remember your goals change, your needs change and as a result, your financial routines may need to change accordingly. The process of developing routines for retirement may not be that different. First establish what your current routines are and determine whether you have good financial habits or bad financial habits. At the same time you can figure out if these habits need to change in retirement or not.

What financial routines do you have and which ones do you think play a role in your financial success? Which of your financial routines might change in retirement?

Financial Success Comes From Working Harder

by Jim Yih

In an article I wrote about how to become a millionaire by 35, I featured an interview with Frugal Trader, the man behind the popular blog Million Dollar Journey. He's a real person on a quest to becoming a millionaire in his 30s. If you did not read this article, you should take a look at it on retirehappy.ca because his thoughts are golden. He did not inherit millions, he is not intending to become a millionaire by winning the lottery or heading to the casino. Instead he is doing it the simple, old fashioned way.

This article was very popular and, if you do read it, you will see from the comments, Million Dollar Journey is a very credible and well respected personal finance blog in Canada. As a result, I was a little surprised when I got an email from a reader who said "I don't want to hear about people who want to do it. Anyone can say they are going to do it. I want to learn from people who have already done it." Despite the sharp tone of his email, there is some merit in his comment so I thought I would respond to his email in this chapter.

After being in the financial industry for the past 23 years, I have met a lot of millionaires in my career and, being the sponge that I am, I have learned from so many of them. And as a result, I have preached what I have learned but I have also practised what I preach and have reached some great financial success myself.

What Was The Key To My Financial Success?

Being the father of four boys, I think a lot about what to teach them to help them find more financial success in life. One thing I tell my boys all the time is that success hinges on working hard and trying your best.

Everything I have in life today comes from working hard. It's very common to hear people preach the merits of working SMARTER and not HARDER. As much as I can appreciate the merits of that message when it comes to time management and productivity, I think we have put too much emphasis on that message and it's created an excuse to be lazy. I always tell people that building wealth is simple, not easy and if you want to build it faster, you have to work harder at it. I believe in this day and age if you are serious about getting ahead and if you want to get serious about accumulating wealth at any age, you have to work SMARTER **and** HARDER. That's what my dad taught me and what I will continue to teach my kids.

You see, I can appreciate Frugal Trader's practical strategies for financial success:

- **Make more than you spend**
- **Make good use of your cash**
- **Know your financial situation**
- **Set goals and take baby steps**

As much as these are prudent strategies and great advice, I'm willing to bet you knew this information already. Knowledge is one thing but taking it the next step and putting ideas to work is really the key. Implementing ideas is where working smarter and harder comes into play.

The key to success lies in your belief, your commitment, your actions, your effort, your discipline, etc. and that's the stuff that's hard.

So What's The Main Reason People Can't Or Won't Become Millionaires?

I think wealth is achievable for anyone and everyone and while circumstances may play a role in attaining wealth, most people can do it by developing good financial habits. For the people who don't get there, perhaps the problem is they don't want it bad enough or they are not willing to work hard enough? Maybe they can't stay disciplined or they are not committed to changing their financial habits? Maybe the key to wealth is really as simple as just doing what it takes to reach your goal.

Implementing Your Financial Goals
by Jim Yih

New Year is a time when people often come up with some new financial resolutions. For some, their focus will be on getting rid of debt. Others will have savings goals. Some people just need to know more about their investments. Many people need to control their spending through budgets. Whatever your goals or resolutions are, the key to success comes from getting it done. As a result, I offer you some key principles to getting your resolutions implemented.

Principles of Implementation

Here are five universal principles of implementing change and getting results. These are principles in my life that I try to live by.

1. **Find Focus and Simplicity**

    The late, great Jim Rohn, profoundly said "There are half a dozen things that make 80% of the difference in anything you do. Focus on those half a dozen things as they will make most of the difference." Far too many people spend too much time on the 20% that has little impact on the outcome. To find focus, you need to set some goals and stay focused on those goals! There's something to be said about keeping it simple!

2. **Change Your Lifestyle**

    Far too often change is temporary. You see this in the gyms right after the New Year. They get really busy for the first couple of months and then things start to slow down again because too many people go back to their old habits. To be successful over the long haul, you must make everlasting changes and the only way you can do that is to change your habits. Steven Covey says it take 21 days to change a habit. In my opinion, it takes 21 months to forever change your financial habits.

3. Just Do It

Nike said it best. You see, I am in the information business. I provide lots of great ideas but ideas are just ideas. The best ideas in the world are the ones that are put to work. They are the implemented ideas. You are better to do and fail then to not do anything at all. And if we think back to point number 1, you are likely to be more successful by doing fewer things that are important and do them well than trying to do too many things poorly. You can have all the information in the world but if you don't do anything with that information, what good is it?

4. Take Responsibility

The hardest thing to do is to recognize that you are responsible for where you are today. It's much easier to blame other people or circumstances but remember, you hold a considerable power. When you do hold yourself accountable, the good news it the future is yours to change! Stop making excuses, stop whining, stop blaming. Get focused on the things you need to do to change and improve and get started. If it help you, find a friend to keep you accountable. Or get and advisor to keep you on track.

5. Stay Disciplined

Life is busy and full of temptations to take us off course. The key firstly is to have a course or a plan or a road map. Once you have the plan, then the motivation to get started, you need the will power to keep it up until it becomes a habit.

Are you ready to commit to these five keys to success?

Conclusion

The end of this book isn't really an ending at all; it's intended to be a beginning. Whether you read it from cover to cover, or whether you dipped in and out, reading only the chapters that resonated with you doesn't really matter. What actually matters is what you do with that information when you close the cover and how you allow it to impact your own situation.

It's said that there are four stages of change:

- Awareness
- Understanding
- Action
- Results

One of the goals of this book is to make you more aware of your own financial situation; your areas of strength and your areas of vulnerability and/or challenge. Once you're aware of those things, you begin to understand how they impact your life in a positive or a negative way and you can decide whether or not to take action to create change.

The action (or inaction) that you choose, leads to your results.

Making a change is rarely the easiest path to take but it is often the most rewarding. Finances and money are sources of challenge and confusion to many people but after reading this book, you know that doesn't have to be the case. Making the decision to take control of your money and apply some of the basic principles of managing (and protecting) money that are discussed in this book can lead, not only to more wealth, but also to increased happiness and reduced stress.

The next step is up to you...

Notes

Notes

Financial Education

Jim is the founder and CEO of his company The Think Box. Think Box specializes in putting financial education programs in the workplace.

Think Box caters to employers who care about the financial well being of their employees. We are the perfect complement to both existing wellness programs, as well as Group Retirement Programs like pensions and Group RRSP programs. We take ordinary Group Retirement Plans and turn them into exceptional ones by providing fun, engaging and unique education programs.

We take employee education and service to a new level. We help employers and their businesses by delivering financial education programs that employees rave about.

For more information, visit www.FinancialEducationCanada.com

Good Research Leads To Good Decisions

Education and knowledge are the roots of financial success. Beyond Jim's articles, presentations and individual consulting, Jim has developed a suite of products to help people achieve more success, wealth and happiness.

Jim is the author of **9 books** including:
o   Mutual Fundamentals I and II
o   Seven Strategies to Guarantee Your Investments
o   Smart Tips for Estate Planning
o   Ideas for Success, Wealth and Happiness
o   A Simple Guide on Guaranteed Investing
o   A Beginners Guide to Saving and Investing
o   Investing is Not Rocket Science

In addition to his books, Jim has developed audio programs, DVDs and software:
o   MONEY Audio Program
o   TAKE CONTROL OF YOUR MONEY DVD
o   My Estate Organizer
o   My Legacy Organizer

To learn more about Jim's books, CDs, videos and software programs, visit his website www.JimYih.com

Made in the USA
Columbia, SC
29 September 2018